Soccer – Passing and Ball (

Soccer –
Passing and Ball Control

84 Drills and Exercises Designed to Improve Passing and Control

Thomas Dooley & Christian Titz

Meyer & Meyer Sport

Photo & Illustration Credits:

Cover Photos: dpa – Picture Alliance, © fotolia, © fotolia/Rainer Claus
Cover Design: Sabine Groten
Illustrations: Easy2Coach Draw

British Library Cataloguing in Publication Data
A catalogue record for this book is available from the British Library

Thomas Dooley & Christian Titz
Soccer – Passing and Ball Control
Maidenhead: Meyer & Meyer Sport (UK) Ltd., 2010
ISBN 978-1-84126-300-7

© 2010 by Meyer & Meyer Sport
Aachen, Adelaide, Auckland, Budapest, Cape Town, Graz, Indianapolis,
Maidenhead, Olten (CH), Singapore, Toronto
Member of the World
Sport Publishers' Association (WSPA)
www.w-s-p-a.org

Printed and bound by: B.O.S.S Druck und Medien GmbH, Germany
ISBN 978-1-84126-300-7
E-Mail: info@m-m-sports.com
www.m-m-sports.com

Table of Contents

Table of Contents

As I first turned my thoughts to writing this training material I was very quickly drawn to the fascination of this topic. Until then, I had never found all the coaching subjects covered in one book. Finally we have such a book. It is impressive how many aspects of coaching in the various chapters are covered with the help of endless exercises and drills. I believe that this book is unique throughout the world and quite simply a must for anyone interested in soccer. We are already experiencing a great deal of success with these coaching concepts.

With the help of this book, this topic is complete. In addition to the book, we offer further books with coaching exercises for differing age groups and many practical, useful tips for coaches and players alike. Personally, for me, it was important that there was something here for everybody. You will notice, when reading closely, that we always speak of the player as 'he'. This form has only been used to simplify the writing process and does, of course, include all female players. Because one thing is clear - this book is aimed at anyone interested in soccer, irrespective of gender.

The symbiosis of practice-related coaching sessions on the pitch through the graphical and text descriptions to the complete application of the drills is facinating. This proves the point that without a structured concept, successful coaching is simply not possible.

Enjoy reading, and learning.

Sincerely,

Thomas Dooley

Learning these skills and movements, with the required timing, takes time and should therefore be repeated regularly in the form of passing exercises and small-sides games.

Exact passing is enormously important for successful soccer. As a result, passing and control has to be practiced regularly. Mistakes must be corrected.

Particularly control with as few touches as possible is trained today all too little, although this skill performed correctly is the difference between keeping and losing the ball.

There are a several ways to pass the ball:
- with the instep
- with the 'laces'
- with the outstep
- with the ball of the foot
- a variation of the ball of the foot techinque is the so-called banana pass which is a pass with large amounts of spin on the ball

When performing a pass, it is important to remember the following:
1. The group should stand several meters away from the coach.
2. The technique should be explained slowly and clearly. First step is to explain in front of the group. Second step, the group should be able to see the technique from behind. (Note: Particularly children can follow a skill better if they see it from this perspective).
3. Start slowly and use both feet.
4. The technique can be learned as a 'dry exercise' so that the players can learn the required techniques and movements.

Aspects of good coaching
- Always demand accuracy and pace (the slow version does not lead to the necessary success in the game).
- Explaining the exercises should not lead to an information overload (lack of concentration leads to additional mistakes). It is important to find the right balance between correcting and allowing the exercises to flow.
- Players should learn (as in the game) to observe and then implement what they observed.
- Always correct the mistakes to assure they do not become automatisms.
- Always address the players with clarity and empathy.
- Advanced groups can be approached simulating game-related stress situations (loud speech, critical comments during the exercise etc.).
- Always demand full concentration.
- The coach's demeanor (body language, tonality, corrections) is a key factor to the quality of the training.

Two fundamental aspects must always be remembered:
1. What are the player's arms doing?
2. What is the player's foot and body posture?

Implementing technique and posture for passing
- The supporting leg should be 30-40 cm next to the ball.
- During the pass with the inside of the foot the tip of the foot points up, the ankle is tight and opened up 90 degrees to the outside. The active leg is slightly lifted and the ball is struck in the center. The body leans over the ball without going into a hollow back.
- The upper body is leaning slightly over the ball.
- The foot is swung downwards.

- The arms are positioned as follows: Passing with the right stretch, the left arm goes toward the right hip, passing with the left stretch, the right arm goes to the left hip.
- Stretch pass: Tip of the foot points downward, ankle is tight.
- When playing the ball with the outside of the foot, leaning back slightly is allowed. The ball is played with the outside toes and outside of the foot, giving it a spin.
- The shot with the inside of the foot: The ball is played with the inside and with the stretch. The standing leg is next to the ball and the player's upper body leans to the side. The toes point downward similar to when taking a stretch shot.
- Spinning pass: The ball is played with the tip of the inside of the foot, giving it a spin. The body leans to the side.
- The player awaiting the pass approaches the passing player and receives the pass while going forward toward the ball. He receives it with one touch or passes it on immediately.
- The pass needs to be played into the path of the player awaiting the ball.
- The player passing has to consider the path of the player awaiting the ball.
- The first movement of the player receiving the pass occurs when the passer takes aim.
- The pass beating the opponent should be played to the correct side. Should a player want to pass to the left of the opponent, he should play a curve around the opponent with the inside of his left foot. If he uses the inside of his right foot to pass to the left instead, the ball is easily intercepted or the path is forced to the side rather than into deep space.
- Due to the high demands on a player's refined technique, the pace of the pass should always be adjusted to the level of the players (children and beginners can start slowly).

Implementing technique and posture for receiving and controlling the ball

- Receiving and controlling the ball should never need more than one touch.
- The ball can either be received with the right or the left, the inside or the outside of the foot.
- The ball has to be controlled by the player the moment it touches the ground. If done properly, the ball does not bounce away and can be controlled by the player directly.
- To avoid the ball bouncing away and to assure a fluent and fast ball reception and control, the player has to have good timing and the right technique to control the ball.
- Using the example of ball reception and control with the inside of the right foot, the motion looks like the player needs to control the ball with the inside of his foot the moment it touches the ground. For this, the leg is swung from right to left into the direction of the ball. The foot is led downward toward the ball (similar to the motion when shooting with just the swing being smaller) stopping the ball from bouncing away. The entire weight of the body is now placed on the left supporting leg; the upper body is turned right from the hip (right shoulder turned back). The eyes are on the ball, which brings the body to lean over the ball as well.
- When receiving and controlling the ball with the outside of the foot, the angle of the foot is opened. The lower leg is bent inward at the knee as well so that the motion of the foot can go from top to bottom toward the right and toward the ball. The ball is struck with the entire outside of the foot.

Alternative:

Ball reception and control from behind the supporting leg toward the left foot. This receiving technique connects the reception with an immediate change in directions to the side. This technique is done with the inside of the foot. It happens with one touch and is fluent. The foot is turned into the direction of the approaching ball. Just before contact is made, the foot is pulled back (just a little slower than the speed of the ball). Now the ball can be received slowly and controlled with the inside at the same time.

The following is a list of criteria which a coach and/or player should be aware of when conducting skills training. The order has no relevance and is merely a list.

1. High reps
2. Correct implementation
3. From easy to difficult
4. Regularity
5. Takes place when the player is in a relaxed condition
6. Leads to competetive exercises
7. Build small groups
8. Good demonstration
9. Individualization (train strong and weak players together)
10. Correction, work in detail
11. Adequate material (balls etc.)
12. Precision before speed
13. Increase speed (from slow to fast)
14. Position-specific
15. Varied
16. Train two-footed
17. Show alternatives
18. Age and development appropriate training
19. If possible, include in every training session
20. Tactic and skills training should be trained separately
21. Observe training conditions (weather, pitch etc) and adjust training accordingly
22. Fun
23. 'Chaining' or 'whole-part-whole method' (first simple passing drills then passing combinations)
24. Praise and correct
25. Include time, space, opponent and partner pressure once the player is proficient in the last 26. 100 – 150 reps

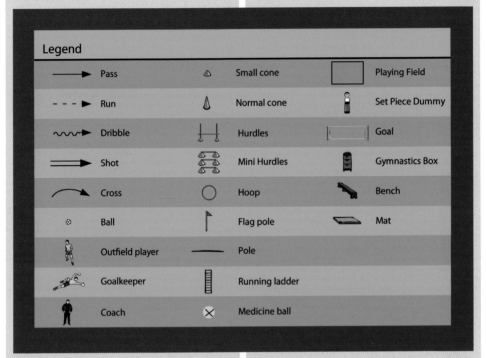

Legend

→	Pass	Small cone			Playing Field
- - ►	Run	Normal cone			Set Piece Dummy
~~►	Dribble	Hurdles			Goal
⇒	Shot	Mini Hurdles			Gymnastics Box
⤴	Cross	Hoop			Bench
Ball		Flag pole			Mat
Outfield player		Pole			
Goalkeeper		Running ladder			
Coach		Medicine ball			

Training Target
- Ball skill (Touch on the ball)

Training Emphasis
- Passing
- Trapping

Training Aspects

Skills involved:	One touch passes, Inside of the laces passing, Inside of the foot passing, Laces, Outside of the foot
Age level:	6 - 14 years
Level of play:	Beginner
Type of training:	Training in pairs
Training structure:	Warm-up, Progression
Purpose:	Improve individual skills
Total number of players:	2 or more players
Participating players:	Whole team
Training location:	Any
Spatial awareness:	Limited playing field
Duration:	10-20 min
Physiology:	Soccer-specific endurance

Organization:
Lay out cone goals as shown. The players stand between the cones.

Process:
The players pass the ball to their partner, standing opposite them, with their right (left) instep. The ball is then controlled with the player's right (left) instep and then passed back, etc.

Alternative:
- The players passes with his right (left) foot. His partner stops the ball with his right (left) instep, passes the ball back with his instep and then runs backwards around a cone.
- Control with one foot, pass with the other. (Tip: Control should be one touch, so that the ball lands at the right (left) foot and can be passed immediately with the next touch.
- Distance between the players 2-3 meters. One touch passing. Instep and outstep.
- Vary with 'laces', crossing technique and outstep.

Tip:
- When controlling the ball, the supporting leg is often too far away from the ball. As a result, the player often leans back. The supporting leg should be 30-40 cm to the side of the ball.
- When passing the ball, the player's foot should be slightly lifted and swung downwards towards the ball.
- Many players control the ball with their 'laces' or outstep. Control with your instep lightly flexed over the ball is, at first, much easier.

Field size:
The practice area is 10 x 15 m and can be varied according to ability.

Cone margins:
The distance between the cones is 10-15 m long, and 5-7 m wide.

Materials:
4 cones or more

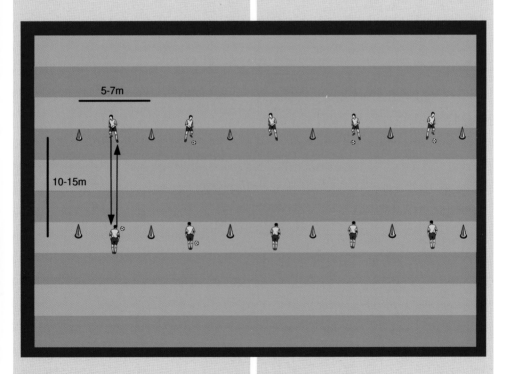

Training Target
- Ball skill (Touch on the ball)

Training Emphasis
- Passing
- Trapping

Training Aspects

Skills involved:	One touch passes, Short passing, Inside of the laces passing, Inside of the foot passing, Laces, Outside of the foot, Trapping, Trapping into space, In motion, Combining technical skill with movement
Age level:	Any age - 14 years
Level of play:	Beginner
Type of training:	Training in pairs
Training structure:	Warm-up, Progression
Purpose:	Improve individual skills
Total number of players:	2 or more players
Participating players:	Whole team
Training location:	Any
Spatial awareness:	Limited playing field
Duration:	10-20 min
Physiology:	Soccer-specific endurance

Organization:
2 players start behind 2 cones 6 - 8m apart and pass the ball to and fro.

Process:
Organization: Both players stand behind their cones. Player A passes the ball in a straight line with his left instep to player B. B lays the ball onto his left foot with his right instep and passes back to A with his left foot. A controls the ball with his right foot and passes back with his left. Note: 1 and 3 are the movement of the ball, 2 and 4 are player movements and control.

Tip:
- Always make sure that the correct feet are used to control and pass the ball.
- Don't forget to train with both feet.
- When controlling the ball, the supporting leg is often too far away from the ball. As a result, the player often leans back. The supporting leg should be 30-40 cm to the side of the ball.
- When passing and controlling the ball, the player's foot should be slightly lifted and swung downwards towards the ball.

Field size:
Practice area for 2 players
8 x 5 m (depending upon player ability and number)

Cone margins:
Distance 8 x 5 m (if training with more than two players.)

Materials:
2 cones or more

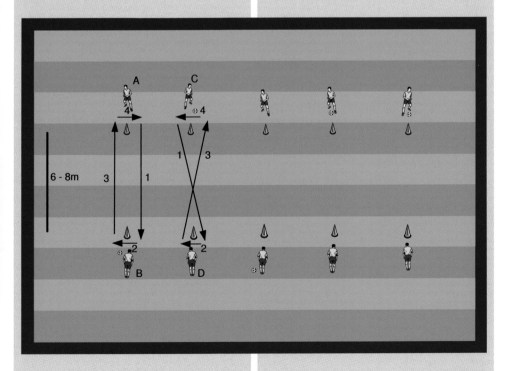

Training Target
- Ball skill (Touch on the ball)

Training Emphasis
- Passing
- Trapping

Training Aspects

Skills involved:	One touch passes, Short passing, Long passing, Inside of the laces passing, Inside of the foot passing, Laces, Outside of the foot, Control, Controlling the ball, In motion, Standing, Combining technical skill with movement
Age level:	Any age
Level of play:	Beginner
Type of training:	Training in pairs
Training structure:	Warm-up, Progression
Purpose:	Improve individual skills
Total number of players:	2 or more players
Participating players:	Whole team
Training location:	Any
Spatial awareness:	Limited playing field
Duration:	10-15 min
Physiology:	Soccer-specific endurance

Organization:
Rectangular cone box, as shown, for 2 players.

Process:
2 players pass the ball to one another.

Alternative:
- Passing with the instep/outstep
- Volley or 'laces' pass
- Passing 'back heel' behind the standing (left/right)
- Control on the chest/head/foot/thigh and then pass back

Tip:
- When completing this drill with more than 2 players, the cones should be laid out equi-distant.
- When controlling the ball, the supporting leg is often too far away from the ball. As a result, the player often leans back. The supporting leg should be 30-40 cm to the side of the ball.
- When passing and controlling the ball, the player's foot should be slightly lifted and swung downwards towards the ball.

Field size:
Short passing
Distance (length): 5-10 m
Distance (width): 4 m
Long passes (on the ground and in the air)
Distance (length): 15-30 m
Distance (width): 6 m

Cone margins:
Distance (length): 5-30 m
DIstance (width): 4-6 m

Materials:
4 cones or more

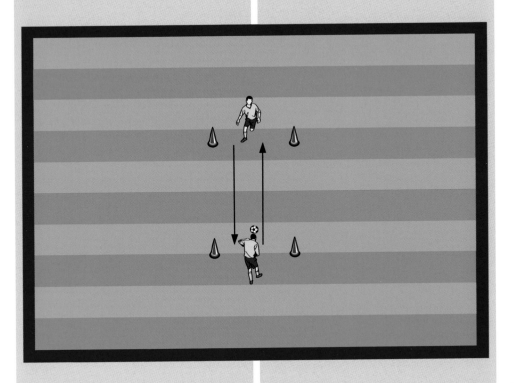

Training Target
- Ball skill (Touch on the ball)

Training Emphasis
- Passing
- Trapping

Training Aspects

Skills involved:	Short passing, Long passing, Inside of the laces passing, Inside of the foot passing, Laces, Outside of the foot, Control, Combining technical skill with movement
Age level:	Any age - 12 years
Level of play:	Beginner
Type of training:	Training in pairs
Training structure:	Warm-up, Progression
Purpose:	Improve individual skills
Total number of players:	2 or more players
Participating players:	Whole team
Training location:	Any
Spatial awareness:	Limited playing field
Duration:	10-20 min
Physiology:	Soccer-specific endurance

Organization:
2 players stand opposite each other next to a cone and pass the ball to one another.

Process:
2 players pass the ball with one or more touches.
Alternative:
- Control with the instep, pass with the outstep.
- 'Laces' and/or crossing technique
- Pass on the ground
- Pass in the air
- Passing with the outstep
- Control a thrown ball from the partner on the head and then pass back with the laces or instep
- Control a thrown ball from the partner on the thigh and then pass back with the laces or instep
- Control a thrown ball from the partner on the chest and then pass back with the laces or instep

Tip:
- This exercise offers many variations.
- When controlling the ball, the supporting leg is often too far away from the ball. As a result, the player often leans back. The supporting leg should be 30-40 cm to the side of the ball.
- When passing the ball the player's foot should be slightly lifted and swung downwards towards the ball.

Field size:
Distance (length/players): 5-8 m
Distance width: 4 m

Cone margins:
Distance: 5-8 m

Materials:
2 cones or more

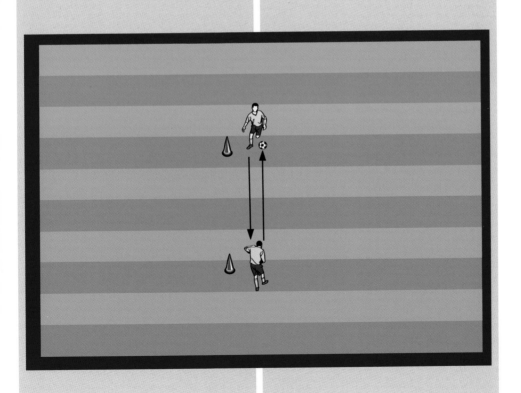

Training Target
- Ball skill (Touch on the ball)

Training Emphasis
- Passing
- Trapping

Training Aspects

Skills involved:	Long passing, Inside of the laces passing, Inside of the foot
Age level:	6 - 12 years
Level of play:	Beginner
Type of training:	Individual training
Training structure:	Progression, Conclusion
Purpose:	Solo training, Improve individual skills
Total number of players:	Player
Participating players:	Whole team
Training location:	Any
Spatial awareness:	Free space
Duration:	10-15 min

Organization:
Several cones are placed at various distances from a small goal. The cones denote the starting position for the player. The distance of the cones from the goal can be reduced/increased depending upon ability.

Process:
The player starts at one of the cones and passes on the ground or in the air into the goal. If it is easy for the player to score, then the distance between the cone and the goal should be increased. Depending upon ability, the player should pass with his right or left front.

There are several techniques for passing a soccer ball:
- with the instep
- with the 'laces'
- with the outstep
- with the crossing technique

Tip:
The exercise can also take the form of a competition with two players. The players pass the ball, one after another, into the goal. The player who has scored the most goals after a set number of tries is the winner.

Important:
- The supporting leg should be 30-40 cm to the side of the ball.
- When passing and controlling with the instep, the passing foot should be lightly lifted to strike the ball in the middle. The player's body should be over the ball and the player should not lean back.
- Swing the foot through after contact.
- Watch the arms! When passing with the right instep, the player's left arm should cross to his right hip and vice versa.
- When passing with the 'laces' the ankle should be opened, toes pointing downwards with the upper body lightly bent over the ball.

- When passing with the outstep, the player can lean back slightly.
- When passing with the crossing technique, the player should approach the ball diagonally leaning slightly to one side.

Field size:
5-20 x 4 m

Cone margins:
Distance from the goal: 5-20 m

Materials:
1 cone, 1 small goal

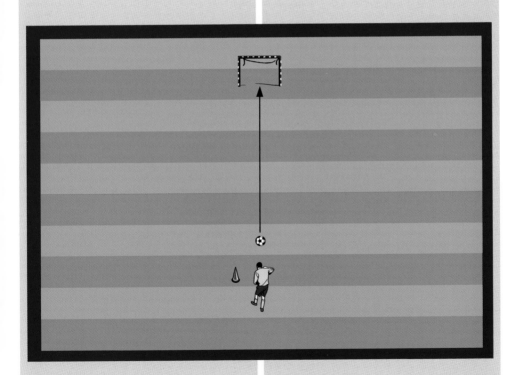

Training Target
- Ball skill (Touch on the ball)

Training Emphasis
- Passing

Training Aspects

Skills involved:	Long passing
Age level:	Any age
Level of play:	Professional
Type of training:	Team training
Training structure:	Conclusion
Purpose:	Training for fun, Improve individual skills
Total number of players:	2 or more players
Participating players:	Whole team
Training location:	Any
Spatial awareness:	Free space
Duration:	10-15 min

Organization:
The player stands next to a cone. The coach (or another player) stands approx. 10-15 meters away for players up to 12 years old and 20 - 35 meters for players 13 and over. The distance should be adjusted depending upon age: the older the player, the greater the distance.

Process:
The player attempts to play a long pass to the coach/partner, without the ball touching the ground.

Alternative:
The pass is played with the instep, with the crossing technique or with the 'laces'. To make make the exercise more difficult, the coach/partner can point in a direction which he would like the ball passed.

Tip:
- For players aged 17 and over the distance can be 30 meters.
- The supporting foot should be 30-40cm to the side of the ball, in line with the ball.
- When passing with the instep, the toes should point upwards, the ankle joint should be tensed and the upper body slightly leaning over the ball.
- Stand on the balls of your feet, the passing foot should be slightly raised to strike the ball in the middle. Bring your body over the ball and don't lean back. (Ball control is achieved using the same technique.)
- The foot should follow through after striking the ball.
- Movement of the arms is important: when passing with the right instep, the left arm should cross to the right hip; when passing with the left instep, the right arm should cross to the left hip.

- The player can lean back slightly when passing with the outstep.
- When passing with the ball of the foot, the player approaches the ball diagonally with his body slightly to the side of the ball.

Field size:
Distance (width): 4-5 m
Distance (length): between 10-35 m depending upon age

Cone margins:
Distance to coach (or partner): 10-35 m

Materials:
1 cone

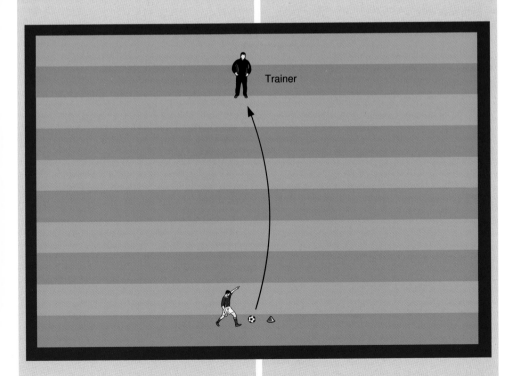

Trainer

Training Target
- Ball skill (Touch on the ball)

Training Emphasis
- Passing

Training Aspects

Skills involved:	One touch passes, Long passing
Age level:	14 years - Adult
Level of play:	Any
Type of training:	Individual training
Training structure:	Progression, Conclusion
Purpose:	Improve individual skills
Total number of players:	Player, 2 or more players
Participating players:	Whole team
Training location:	Any
Spatial awareness:	Penalty box
Duration:	10-15 min

Organization:
The player stands at the edge of the 18 yard box with a ball. A small goal is placed inside a normal goal.

Process:
The player attempts to shoot the ball between the crossbar of the small goal and the crossbar of the normal goal.

Alternative:
- The distance from the goal can be increased by placing a cone farther back.
- This exercise can also take the form of a competition. Two or more players take turns, he who scores the most goals, wins.

There are a several ways to pass the ball:
- with the instep
- with the 'laces'
- with the outstep
- with the ball of the foot
- the banana shot

Tip:
- The supporting foot should be 30-40cm to the side of the ball, in line with the ball.
- When passing with the instep, the toes should point upwards, the ankle joint should be tensed and the upper body slightly leaning over the ball.
- Stand on the balls of your feet, the passing foot should be slightly raised to strike the ball in the middle. Bring your body over the ball and don't lean back. (Ball control is achieved using the same technique.)
- The foot should follow through after striking the ball.
- Movement of the arms is important: when passing with the right instep, the left arm should cross to the right hip; when passing with the left instep, the right arm should cross to the left hip.
- The player can lean back slightly when passing with the outstep.
- When passing with the ball of the foot, the player approaches the ball diagonally with his body slightly to the side of the ball

Field size:
18 yard box

Cone margins:
Distance from goal: up to 20 m

Materials:
1 normal goal, 1 cone, 1 small goal

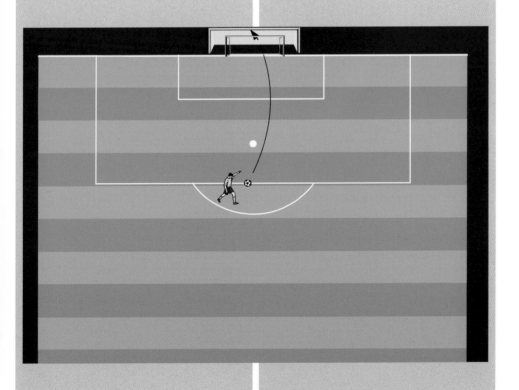

Training Target
- Ball skill (Touch on the ball)

Training Emphasis
- Passing

Training Aspects

Skills involved:	One touch passes, Long passing
Age level:	13 years - Adult
Level of play:	Any
Type of training:	Individual training
Training structure:	Progression, Conclusion
Purpose:	Improve individual skills
Total number of players:	Player, 2 or more players
Participating players:	Whole team
Training location:	Any
Spatial awareness:	Penalty box
Duration:	10-15 min

Organization:
The player stands at the edge of the 18 yard box with a ball. A small goal is placed inside a normal goal.

Process:
The player attempts to shoot the ball between the posts of the small goal and the posts of the normal goal.

Alternative:
- The distance from the goal can be increased by placing a cone farther back.
- This exercise can also take the form of a competition. Two or more players take turns, he who scores the most goals, wins.

There are a several ways to pass the ball:
- with the instep
- with the 'laces'
- with the outstep
- with the ball of the foot
- the banana shot

Tip:
- The supporting foot should be 30-40cm to the side of the ball, in line with the ball.
- When passing with the instep, the toes should point upwards, the ankle joint should be tensed and the upper body slightly leaning over the ball.
- Stand on the balls of your feet, the passing foot should be slightly raised to strike the ball in the middle. Bring your body over the ball and don't lean back. (Ball control is achieved using the same technique.)
- The foot should follow through after striking the ball.
- Movement of the arms is important: when passing with the right instep, the left arm should cross to the right hip; when passing with the left instep, the right arm should cross to the left hip.
- The player can lean back slightly when passing with the outstep.
- When passing with the ball of the foot, the player approaches the ball diagonally with his body slightly to the side of the ball.

Field size:
18 yard box

Cone margins:
Distance from goal: up to 20 m

Materials:
1 normal goal, 1 cones, 1 small goal

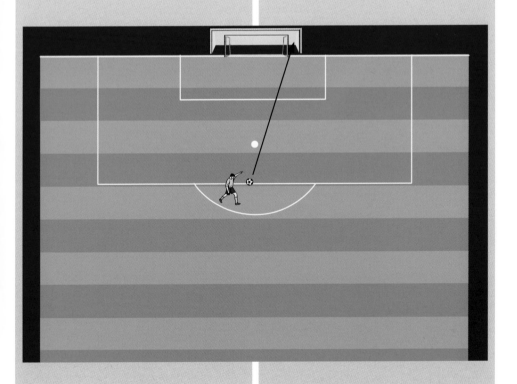

Training Target
- Ball skill (Touch on the ball)

Training Emphasis
- Passing
- Trapping
- Ball control

Training Aspects

Skills involved:	Short passing, Long passing, Trapping
Age level:	9 years - Adult
Level of play:	Any
Type of training:	Group training, Team training
Training structure:	Progression, Main point/Emphasis
Purpose:	Improve individual skills
Total number of players:	12 players, 13 or more players
Participating players:	Whole team
Training location:	Any
Spatial awareness:	Limited playing field
Duration:	10-20 min
Physiology:	Soccer-specific endurance

Organization:
Three boxes (each 10 x 10m) are set up next to one another using 8 cones, as shown.

Process:
There are four player in each box. The players in the middle box try to block the passes played from the players in the outer boxes. Every player in the outer boxes has a ball. The players in the outer boxes try to pass the balls to the players in the outher outer box. If a player in the middle box blocks a pass, he can then come out of the middle zone and changes place with the player who pass the stray ball.

Alternative:
More than 12 players can take part. There are a several ways to pass the ball:
- with the instep
- with the 'laces'
- with the outstep
- with the ball of the foot
- the banana shot

Tip:
- The players in the middle box should be watched closely by the players in the outer boxes and the players in the outer boxes should communicate by calling or with eye contact with their partners in the other outer box.
- The timing of the pass is decisive.
- The supporting foot should be 30-40cm to the side of the ball, in line with the ball.
- When passing with the instep, the toes should point upwards, the ankle joint should be tensed and the upper body slightly leaning over the ball.
- Stand on the balls of your feet, the passing foot should be slightly raised to strike the ball in the middle. Bring your body over the ball and don't lean back. (Ball control is achieved using the same technique.)
- The foot should follow through after striking the ball.
- Movement of the arms is important: when passing with the right instep the left arm should cross to the right hip; when

passing with the left instep the right arm
should cross to the left hip.
- The player can lean back slightly when
passing with the outstep.
- When passing with the ball of the foot,
the player approaches the ball diagonally
with his body slightly to the side of the
ball.

Field size:
30 x 10 m (each box 10 x 10 m)

Cone margins:
Distance (horizontal/vertical): 10 m

Materials:
8 cones

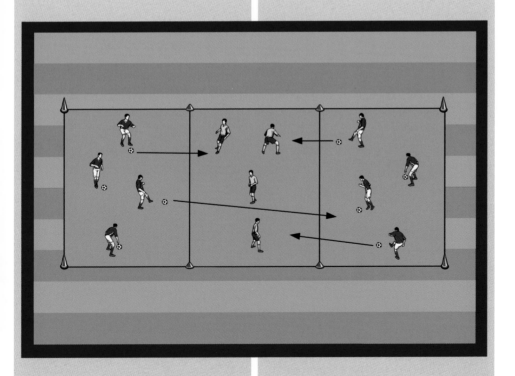

Training Target
- Ball skill (Touch on the ball)

Training Emphasis
- Passing
- Trapping

Training Aspects

Skills involved:	One touch passes, Inside of the laces passing, Inside of the foot passing, Laces
Age level:	9 - 14 years
Level of play:	Any
Type of training:	Group training, Team training
Training structure:	Warm-up, Progression
Purpose:	Training for fun, Improve individual skills
Total number of players:	8 or more players
Participating players:	Whole team
Training location:	Any
Spatial awareness:	Limited playing field
Duration:	10-15 min

Organization:
The field is approx 15 x 20. Pairs are selcted and the pairs stand opposite each other 15m apart.

Process:
Strikeball - the players pass the balls to one another. One ball between two. The blue players try to pass through the channel as often as possible without the red players hitting their balls.

Alternative:
Channel passes could be practiced in pairs as preparation for this exercise.

Tip:
- The timing of the pass is often incorrect (passed too soon or to late).
- The supporting foot should be 30-40cm to the side of the ball, in line with the ball.
- When passing with the instep, the toes should point upwards, the ankle joint should be tensed and the upper body slightly leaning over the ball.

- Stand on the balls of your feet, the passing foot should be slightly raised to strike the ball in the middle. Bring your body over the ball and don't lean back. (Ball control is achieved using the same technique.)
- The foot should follow through after striking the ball.
- Movement of the arms is important: when passing with the right instep, the left arm should cross to the right hip; when passing with the left instep, the right arm should cross to the left hip.
- The player can lean back slightly when passing with the outstep.
- When passing with the ball of the foot, the player approaches the ball diagonally with his body slightly to the side of the ball.

Field size:
15 x 20 m box marked out with cones

Cone margins:
Distance vertical: 15 m
Distance horizontal: 20 m

Materials:
4 cones

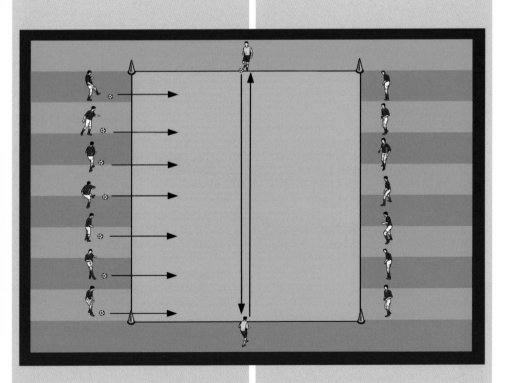

Training Target
- Ball skill (Touch on the ball)

Training Emphasis
- Passing
- Trapping

Training Aspects

Skills involved:	One touch passes, Passing over multiple stations, Short passing, Controlling the ball, In motion
Age level:	6 years - Adult
Level of play:	Advanced
Type of training:	Group training, Team training
Training structure:	Progression
Purpose:	Groups, Improve individual skills
Total number of players:	12 players, 13 or more players
Participating players:	Whole team
Training location:	Any
Spatial awareness:	Limited playing field
Duration:	10-20 min
Physiology:	Soccer-specific endurance

Organization:
Set up a box 30 x 25m. 12 players take up their place in the box and each player has a number from 1 - 12.

Process:
Players 1 and 7 take up their start positions and each has a ball. They pass the ball to the player with the next highest number, i.e. player 1 passes to 2, 2 passes to 3, 3 passes to 4 etc. At the same time player 7 passes to 8, 8 passes to 9, etc.

At the start of the drill each player has at least 2 touches (not one touch). As the drill progresses the drill can be done with one touch.

Alternative:
- Players 1, 5 and 9 each start with a ball (in total 3 balls).
- The number of players and balls is variable. However the level of difficulty varies accordingly.

There are a several ways to pass the ball:
- with the instep
- with the 'laces'
- with the outstep
- with the ball of the foot
- the banana shot (a pass with lots of swerve)

Tip:
- Precise, exact passing is extremely important for successful soccer. As a result passing should be regularly practised. It is important not to forget to correct mistakes and give correct demonstrations.
- The players need good timing as they need to control the ball and pass the ball on. Concentration and eye-contact between the passer and the player receiving are important here.
- The players should call the player receiving the ball before every pass.
- The players should always be on the move and shouldn't occupy the same space. That way the game flows and awareness of space and game intelligence can be improved.

Field size:
Box 30 x 25 m

Cone margins:
30 x 25 m

Materials:
4 cones

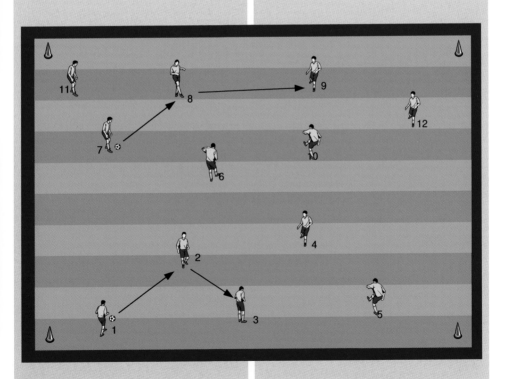

Training Target
- Ball skill (Touch on the ball)

Training Emphasis
- Passing
- Trapping

Training Aspects

Skills involved:	One touch passes, Short passing, Laces, Inside of the foot, Volley, Trapping, Trapping into space, In motion, Combining technical skill with movement, Heading from a standstill, Heading from a jump
Age level:	9 years - Adult
Level of play:	Beginner, Advanced
Type of training:	Group training
Training structure:	Warm-up, Progression, Main point/Emphasis
Purpose:	Improve individual skills
Total number of players:	3 players
Participating players:	Whole team
Training location:	Any
Spatial awareness:	Limited playing field
Duration:	10-20 min
Physiology:	Soccer-specific endurance

Organization:
Three cones in a line at a distance of 5-8 meters. A player stands at each cone.

Process:
Passing between the three players. The middle player comes slightly towards the outer players, receives the pass and then lays the ball back with his first touch. He then turns 180° and moves towards the other outer player and receives the next pass from him.

Alternative:
The following passing combinations are possible:
- Control with the instep and then pass
- Control and turn and pass to the other player
- Pass with the 'laces' and/or ball of the foot (cross technique)
- One touch volley, thrown ball
- One touch with the laces, instep or outstep

- Control on the head, pass back
- Control on the thigh, pass back
- Control on the chest, pass back

Tip:
- Correct mistakes and give sound demonstrations.
- Precision is more important than speed. The tempo can be increased only when the passes reach their destinations.
- When the tempo has been raised, the player can be set under time pressure by the other players.
- If the exercise is done for too long, the players can lose their concentration resulting in mistakes. As a result the players should change positions every 60 seconds.
- The supporting foot should be 30-40cm to the side of the ball, in line with the ball.
- When passing with the instep, the toes should point upwards, the ankle joint should be tensed and the upper body slightly leaning over the ball.

- Stand on the balls of your feet, the passing foot should be slightly raised to strike the ball in the middle. Bring your body over the ball and don't lean back. (Ball control is achieved using the same technique).
- The foot should follow through after striking the ball.
- Movement of the arms is important: when passing with the right instep the left arm should cross to the right hip; when passing with the left instep the right arm should cross to the left hip.
- The player can lean back slightly when passing with the outstep.
- When passing with the ball of the foot, the player approaches the ball diagonally with his body slightly to the side of the ball.

Field size:
Distance vertical: 10-16 m
Distance horizontal: 4-5 m

Cone margins:
Distance between every cone 5-8 m

Materials:
3 cones

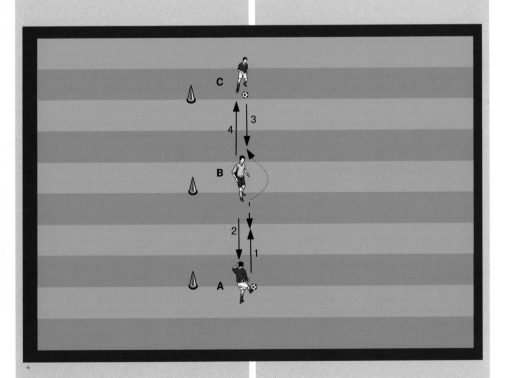

Training Target
- Ball skill (Touch on the ball)

Training Emphasis
- Passing

Training Aspects

Skills involved:	One touch passes, Short passing, Long passing
Age level:	Under 12 years - Adult
Level of play:	Any
Type of training:	Group training
Training structure:	Warm-up, Progression, Main point/Emphasis
Purpose:	Improve individual skills
Total number of players:	3 players
Participating players:	Whole team
Training location:	Any
Spatial awareness:	Limited playing field
Duration:	10-15 min
Physiology:	Soccer-specific endurance

Process:

Passing between the three players. A passes on the ground to B, who comes to receive the ball and lays the ball back to A then passes a long ball to C who lays the ball off to B. B then lays the ball back to B who passes a long ball back to A. This pattern can be repeated as often as required.

Tip:

- Precise, exact passing is extremely important for successful soccer. As a result passing should be regularly practiced. It is important not to forget to correct mistakes and give correct demonstrations.
- This exercise requires a high pass precision.
- The player in the middle will tire after continued play. As a result the players should change positions every 60 seconds.

Further important characteristics:

- The supporting foot should be 30-40cm to the side of the ball, in line with the ball.
- When passing with the instep, the toes should point upwards, the ankle joint should be tensed and the upper body slightly leant over the ball.
- Stand on the balls of your feet, the passing foot should be slightly raised to strike the ball in the middle. Bring your body over the ball and don't lean back. (Ball control is achieved using the same technique).
- The foot should follow through after striking the ball.
- Movement of the arms is important: When passing with the right instep the left arm should cross to the right hip; when passing with the left instep the right arm should cross to the left hip.
- The player can lean back slightly when passing with the outstep.
- When passing with the ball of the foot, the player approaches the ball diagonally with his body slightly to the side of the ball.

Field size:
Distance horizontal: 10-16 m
Distance vertical: 4 m

Cone margins:
Distance 5-8 m

Materials:
3 cones

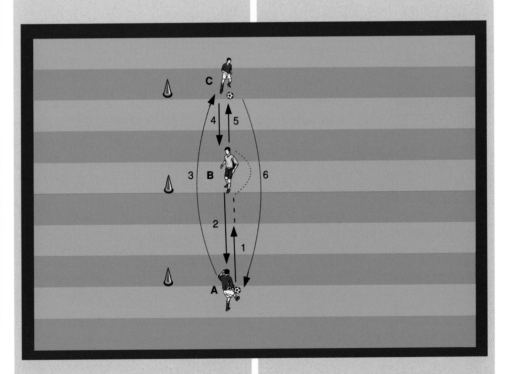

Training Target
- **Ball skill (Touch on the ball)**

Training Emphasis
- **Passing**

Training Aspects

Skills involved:	One touch passes, Passing over multiple stations, Passing in a square, Short passing, Long passing, In motion
Age level:	13 years - Adult
Level of play:	Advanced, Professional
Type of training:	Group training
Training structure:	Warm-up, Progression, Main point/Emphasis
Purpose:	Groups, Improve individual skills
Total number of players:	6 players
Participating players:	Whole team
Training location:	Any
Spatial awareness:	Limited playing field
Duration:	10-20 min
Physiology:	Soccer-specific endurance

Organization:
6 cones make up a rectangluar playing area with 3 cones down each long side.

Process:
Player movement:
Passes 1 -4 within the groups A,B,C and D,E,F take place as shown. A takes up the former position from B (middle cone) after his pass. Player B runs to position C and player C runs towards player A, plays the ball diagonally to D and finally takes up A's former position. The passes in the D,E,F group take place simultaneously and in the same order as the A,B,C group.

After the fourth pass the ball should return to the first player in the other group. The drill now continues with the same pass and move routine as before.

Alternative:
First run the drill with only one ball and then later synchronize the drill with two balls.

Tip:
The exercise should flow clockwise and anti-clockwise. Precision is more important than pass power is the motto of this exercise. The tempo of changing positions in this exercise should only be increased when the passes reach their intended targets regularly.

The players should communicate at all times and awareness of space and speed should be developed and appreciated so that the drill flows.

Further important characteristics:
- The supporting foot should be 30-40cm to the side of the ball, in line with the ball.
- When passing with the instep, the toes should point upwards, the ankle joint should be tensed and the upper body slightly leant over the ball.
- Stand on the balls of your feet, the passing foot should be slightly raised to strike the ball in the middle. Bring your body over the ball and don't lean back. (Ball control is achieved using the same technique).

- The foot should follow through after striking the ball.
- Movement of the arms is important: When passing with the right instep, the left arm should cross to the right hip; when passing with the left instep the right arm should cross to the left hip.
- The player can lean back slightly when passing with the outstep.
- When passing with the ball of the foot, the player approaches the ball diagonally with his body slightly to the side of the ball.

Field size:
15 x 15 m rectangle

Cone margins:
At the side with 3 cones:
Distance between the cones: 7.5 m
At the side with 2 cones:
Distance between cones: 15 m

Materials:
6 cones

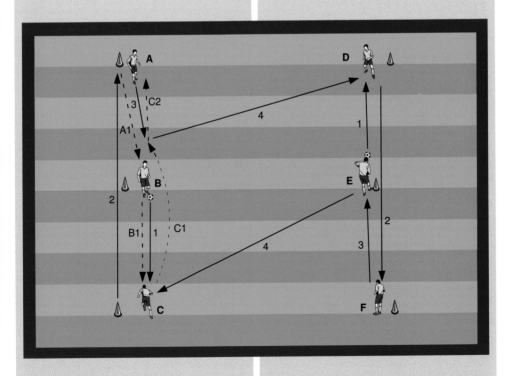

Training Target
- Ball skill (Touch on the ball)

Training Emphasis
- Passing
- Trapping
- Dribbling

Training Aspects

Skills involved:	One touch passes, Wall passes, Short passing, Overlapping, Speed in change of direction
Age level:	Under 8 - 16 years
Level of play:	Beginner, Advanced
Type of training:	Group training
Training structure:	Warm-up, Progression, Main point/Emphasis
Purpose:	Improve individual skills
Total number of players:	6 or more players
Participating players:	Whole team
Training location:	Any
Spatial awareness:	Limited playing field
Duration:	10-20 min
Physiology:	Soccer-specific endurance

Organization:
6 cones are laid out as shown. It is recommended to use large cones for the outer cones or flags (see graphic). The advantage with this is that the players then have to run around the cones/flags and cannot jump over them or cut the corners.

6 players stand opposite each other at a distance of 15-20 meters. The exercise is suitable for 6-10 players.

Process:
A passes on the ground or in the air to B. Player B lays the ball off to the side for A to run on to. A dribbles to the cone and around B then to the large cone/flag and then dribbles back to the other group. After running with the ball the player joins the back of the red group.

The red and blue groups complete the exercise at the same time in opposite directions (as shown).

Alternative:
This exercise can take place in the form of a competition. Both groups start at the same time as described. One team receives a point when their player reaches the opposing team first. The team with the most points is the winner.

Tip:
Note: The players must keep their eye on the other players at all times so that they don't get in each others way.

- The timing of the passes and the player runs often doesn't fit. The players either pas too early or too late.
- The player waiting for the ball should always make a short, dynamic dummy run away from the ball before receiving the pass.
- When laying the ball off the foot should be lifted slightly.
- Hard and exact passes.
- The player often runs faster than he passes.

Field size:
20-20 m

Cone margins:
Small cones
Distance vertical: 10-15 m
Distance horizontal: 5 m
Large cones
Distance vertical: 20 m
Distance horizontal: 20 m
Distance layoff: 7.5 m

Materials:
6 cones

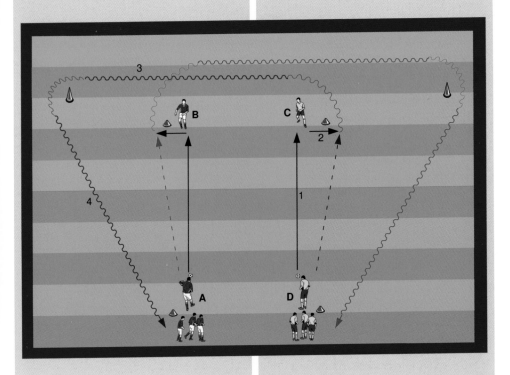

Training Target
- Ball skill (Touch on the ball)

Training Emphasis
- Passing
- Trapping
- Ball control

Training Aspects

Skills involved:	One touch passes, Short passing, Long passing
Age level:	9 - 16 years
Level of play:	Beginner, Advanced
Type of training:	Group training
Training structure:	Warm-up, Progression, Main point/Emphasis
Purpose:	Improve individual skills
Total number of players:	4 players
Participating players:	Whole team
Training location:	Any
Spatial awareness:	Limited playing field
Duration:	10-15 min
Physiology:	Soccer-specific endurance

Organization:
Three boxes are created using 8 cones, with each zone the same size. The cones denote the imaginary lines separating the zones.

Process:
The two blue players pass the ball to one another in their zone as long as they like. It is their aim to get the ball past the red player in the middle zone to the single blue player in the end zone. If they achieve this, the blue player who played the cross-field ball follows his pass and the same exercise starts anew in the end zone.

The red player tries to block and collect the passes through intelligent movement and awareness of space, however he is not allowed to enter the opponents' zone.

Motivation for the red player:
The player in the middle zone is changed at regular intervals. If the red player manages to intercept a pass intended for a blue player, he wins.

Alternative:
To improve awareness the outer cones could be replaced with flags or larger cones.

Tip:
It is recommended that the players play with both feet. At first the passes should be played along the ground. Advanced players can attept to lob the ball over the 'piggie' in the middle.
Coach the red and the blue players in the end zones.

Precise, exact passing is extremely important for successful soccer. As a result passing should be regularly practiced. It is important not to forget to correct mistakes and give correct demonstrations.

- The supporting foot should be 30-40cm to the side of the ball, in line with the ball.
- When passing with the instep, the toes should point upwards, the ankle joint should be tensed and the upper body slightly leaning over the ball.

- Stand on the balls of your feet, the passing foot should be slightly raised to strike the ball in the middle. Bring your body over the ball and don't lean back. (Ball control is achieved using the same technique).
- The foot should follow through after striking the ball.
- Movement of the arms is important: When passing with the right instep, the left arm should cross to the right hip; when passing with the left instep, the right arm should cross to the left hip.
- The player can lean back slightly when passing with the outstep.
- When passing with the ball of the foot, the player approaches the ball diagonally with his body slightly to the side of the ball.

Field size:
18 x 6 m rectangular box. Each zone is 6 x 6 m.

Cone margins:
Distance horizontal: 6 m
Distance vertical: 6 m

Materials:
8 cones

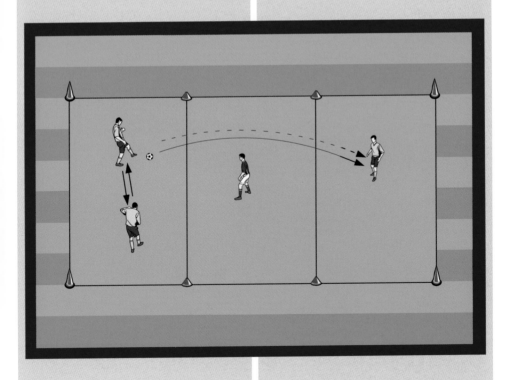

Training Target
- Ball skill (Touch on the ball)

Training Emphasis
- Passing
- Trapping
- Ball control

Training Aspects

Skills involved:	Short passing, Long passing
Age level:	13 years - Adults
Level of play:	Advanced
Type of training:	Team training, Large group training
	8-16 players
Training structure:	Progression, Main point/Emphasis
Purpose:	Part of a team
Total number of players:	10 or more players
Participating players:	Whole team
Training location:	Any
Spatial awareness:	Limited playing field
Duration:	10-25 min
Physiology:	Soccer-specific endurance

Organization:
10 cones make up a 34 x 40 meter field (width of the 18 yard box) with 4 zones (A-D). The 8 blue players are a team and the 8 red players make up one team. There are four players in each zone (see graphic) whereby each team only occupies two zones.

Process:
The blue players in zone A try to pass the ball to their teammates in zone C (and vice-versa). The red players in zone B try to intercept the passes using clever awareness of space and movement. No player can leave his zone. If red intercepts the ball, they then have to try and keep the ball and the blue players in zone C become defenders and must try to intercept the through-balls. The groups of four in each zone should regularly change places.

It is important to change from offense to defense as quickly as possible. The team with the ball should use the whole width of the field to make it as hard as possible for the defending team to intercept the ball.

Tip:
- Arriving passes or interceptins can be counted.
- Exact passing should always be trainined in game-realistic situations.
- Coach game overview/awareness.
- Communication and encouragement.
- The players should stay moving.

Field size:
34 x 40 m field divided into four
8.5 x 40 m zones.

Cone margins:
Distance vertical: 8.5 m
Distance horizontal: 40 m

Materials:
10 cones

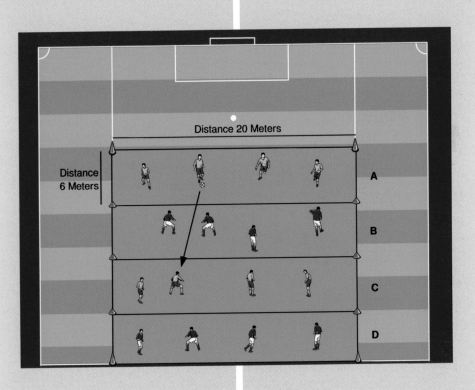

Training Target
- Ball skill (Touch on the ball)

Training Emphasis
- Passing
- Ball control

Training Aspects

Skills involved:	Passing in a square, Short passing, Inside of the foot passing, Trapping, In motion
Age level:	9 years - Adult
Level of play:	Beginner, Advanced
Type of training:	Training in pairs
Training structure:	Warm-up, Progression, Main point/Emphasis
Purpose:	Improve individual skills
Total number of players:	2 players
Participating players:	Whole team
Training location:	Any
Spatial awareness:	Limited playing field
Duration:	10-15 min
Physiology:	Soccer-specific endurance

Organization:
4 cones make up a game box. One player stands at the bottom right hand corner and one at the top left, diagonally across from each one other.

Process:
Both players pass the ball vertically (up the line) to the opposite cone and run immediately horizontally to receive the pass from the other player.

Alternative:
To simplify the drill, the players can control the ball first before passing.

Tip:
The exercise only works if the passes and the runs are timed correctly. The players should aim to build up a rhythm. Both players should pass with both feet.

- Precise, exact passing is extremely important for successful soccer. As a result passing should be regularly practiced. It is important not to forget to correct mistakes and give correct demonstrations.
- The supporting foot should be 30-40cm to the side of the ball, in line with the ball.
- When passing with the instep, the toes should point upwards, the ankle joint should be tensed and the upper body slightly leaning over the ball.
- Stand on the balls of your feet, the passing foot should be slightly raised to strike the ball in the middle. Bring your body over the ball and don't lean back. (Ball control is achieved using the same technique).
- The foot should follow through after striking the ball.
- Movement of the arms is important: When passing with the right instep, the left arm should cross to the right hip; when passing with the left instep, the right arm should cross to the left hip.

- The player can lean back slightly when passing with the outstep.
- When passing with the ball of the foot, the player approaches the ball diagonally with his body slightly to the side of the ball.

Field size:
10 x 10 m box

Cone margins:
Distance between the cones: 10 m

Materials:
4 cones

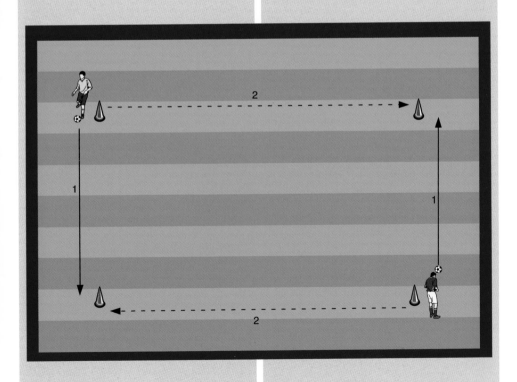

Training Target
- Ball skill (Touch on the ball)

Training Emphasis
- Passing
- Trapping

Training Aspects

Skills involved:	One touch passes
Age level:	9 years - Adult
Level of play:	Any
Type of training:	Group training
Training structure:	Warm-up, Progression, Main point/Emphasis
Purpose:	Improve individual skills
Total number of players:	5 players, 6 players
Participating players:	Whole team
Training location:	Any
Spatial awareness:	Limited playing field
Duration:	10-20 min
Physiology:	Soccer-specific endurance, Speed endurance, Power & Speed

Organization:
4 cones make up the playing field. At least 5 and maximum 6 players are needed for this exercise. 2 players stand at the start cone and one players starts at each of the other three cones.

Process:
All passes should be one-touch (in the order shown). Each player should follow his pass. As a result the drill turns, the drill can run clockwise or counterclockwise. The player waiting for the ball should make a small, dynamic dummy run away from the ball before receiving each pass.

Alternative:
- The players can take more touches, i.e. they can control the ball before passing. Normally the first touch should bring the ball under control and the second touch should be the pass.
- 2 balls and 6 players.

Tip:
The exercise can be run with one ball or with two depending upon player skill level. When playing with two balls, the balls must start diagonally apart from one another. The diagonally opposite positions must be occupied by at least 2 players.

The player waiting for the ball makes his move as the previous player controls the ball.

The supporting leg should not be too far from the ball, and make sure that the players don't lean back.

Further Important characteristics:
The supporting foot should be 30-40cm to the side of the ball, in line with the ball.

- When passing with the instep, the toes should point upwards, the ankle joint should be tensed and the upper body slightly leaning over the ball.

- Stand on the balls of your feet, the passing foot should be slightly raised to strike the ball in the middle. Bring your body over the ball and don't lean back. (Ball control is achieved using the same technique).
- The foot should follow through after striking the ball.
- Movement of the arms is important: When passing with the right instep, the left arm should cross to the right hip; when passing with the left instep, the right arm should cross to the left hip.
- The player can lean back slightly when passing with the outstep.
- When passing with the ball of the foot, the player approaches the ball diagonally with his body slightly to the side of the ball.

Field size:
12 x 12 m box

Cone margins:
Distance between the cones: 12 m

Materials:
4 cones

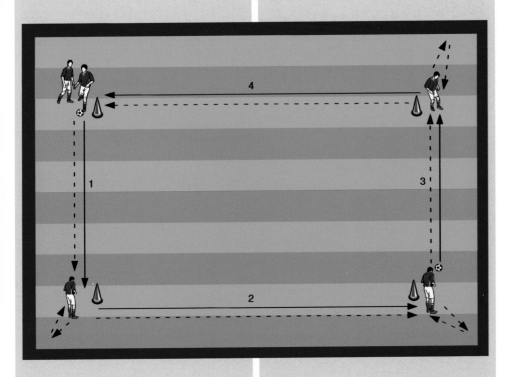

Training Target
- Ball skill (Touch on the ball)

Training Emphasis
- Passing

Training Aspects

Skills involved:	One touch passes
Age level:	Under 12 - 16 years
Level of play:	Beginner, Advanced
Type of training:	Group training
Training structure:	Warm-up, Progression, Main point/Emphasis
Purpose:	Improve individual skills
Total number of players:	4 players
Participating players:	Whole team
Training location:	Any
Spatial awareness:	Limited playing field
Duration:	10-15 min
Physiology:	Soccer-specific endurance

Organization:
Two cone goals are set up next to each other. 2 pairs of players stand opposite each other on either side of each cone goal. One ball per player. The players are 12 meters apart.

Process:
All four players pass their balls at the same time through the cone goal and run to the horizontaly placed cone to receive the on-coming pass and to then pass the ball back through the cone goal with the right timing.

Alternative:
To make the exercise more difficult, the cone goals can be set closer together and/or the length of the passes can be increased.

Tip:
Pass and movement timing is important to ensure that the exercise runs smoothly. Both feet should be used.

Further important characteristics:
- The supporting foot should be 30-40cm to the side of the ball, in line with the ball.
- When passing with the instep, the toes should point upwards, the ankle joint should be tensed and the upper body slightly leaning over the ball.
- Stand on the balls of your feet, the passing foot should be slightly raised to strike the ball in the middle. Bring your body over the ball and don't lean back. (Ball control is achieved using the same technique).
- The foot should follow through after striking the ball.
- Movement of the arms is important: when passing with the right instep the left arm should cross to the right hip; when passing with the left instep the right arm should cross to the left hip.
- The player can lean back slightly when passing with the outstep.
- When passing with the ball of the foot, the player approaches the ball diagonally with his body slightly to the side of the ball.

Field size:
12 x 12 m

Cone margins:
Distance between the two cone goals:
2 m
Distance between the two inner cones:
8 m

Materials:
4 cones

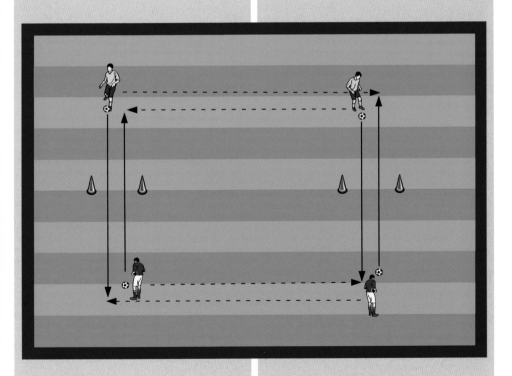

Training Target
- Ball skill (Touch on the ball)

Training Emphasis
- Dribbling

Training Aspects

Skills involved:	Short passing, Controlling the ball, Dribbling
Age level:	6 - 16 years
Level of play:	Any
Type of training:	Group training
Training structure:	Progression
Purpose:	Improve individual skills
Total number of players:	5 players, 6 players
Participating players:	Whole team
Training location:	Any
Spatial awareness:	Limited playing field
Duration:	10-15 min
Physiology:	Soccer-specific endurance, Speed endurance, Power & Speed

Organization:
A rectangle is formed with 4 cones. Two players stand at the start position with a ball, one player starts at each of the other cones.

Process:
There are two variations of this drill.

Variation 1:
5 players, 1 ball.
Player A sprints towards player B. At the cone player B takes the ball off A at top speed and sprints diagonally to player C. The drill then continues as before (see graphic). Each pass should take place at a distance of 1 -2m.

Variation 2:
6 players, 2 balls
The drill is the same as variation 1. The two balls start diagonally apart from one another and these cones should be occupied by at least 2 players. It makes sense to try this variation after the players have successfully mastered variation 1.

Tip:
- The ball should not be further thann 50cm from the foot when dribbling. Make sure the players take small steps.
- Precision is more important than speed.
- It is advisable to drible with the outstep and then use the instep to correct dribbling when needed.
- The ball should not be passed too hard during the 'take'.
- The player awaiting the ball should stand showing his team mate on which foot he would like to receive the pass.
- The player awaiting the ball should start moving towards the ball when the passer has recieved the ball.
- The supporting leg is often too far away from the ball and/or the player leans back.
- When passing the foot should be slightly lifted and swung downwards lightly towards the ball.
- Many players control and drivbble the ball with their 'laces'. Controlling the ball with the instep is much easier as a first step.

Field size:
12 x 12 m

Cone margins:
Distance between the cones: 12 m

Materials:
4 cones

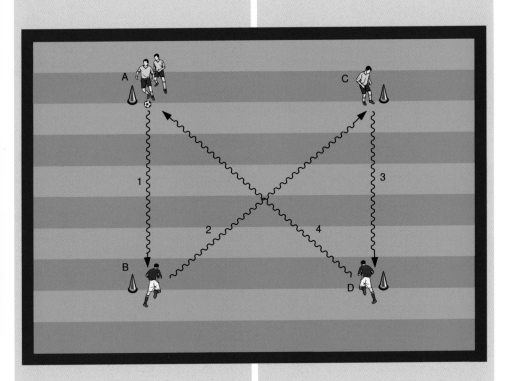

Training Target
- Ball skill (Touch on the ball)

Training Emphasis
- Passing, Ball control
- Trapping
- Dribbling

Training Aspects

Skills involved:	Short passing, Dribbling
Age level:	9 years - Adult
Level of play:	Advanced, Professional
Type of training:	Group training, Team training
Training structure:	Progression, Main point/Emphasis
Purpose:	Improve individual skills
Total number of players:	5 players, 6 players
Participating players:	Whole team
Training location:	Any
Spatial awareness:	Limited playing field
Duration:	10-15 min
Physiology:	Speed endurance, Power & Speed

Organization:
Set up a box with 4 cones. Two players start at the first cone, all the other cones have one player.

Process:
5 players, 1 ball
Player A passes the ball to player B and follows his pass. Player B sprints diagonally with the ball to player C who performs a take. Player C controls the ball and passes to player D. D then dribbles, as before diagonally. The process should flow in both directions.

Alternative:
6 players, 1 ball
The drill must start at the diagonally opposite cones, these cones must be occupied by at least 2 players.

Tip:
- The ball should not be further thann 50cm from the foot when dribbling. Make sure the players take small steps.
- Precision is more important than speed.
- It is advisable to drible with the outstep and then use the instep to correct dribbling when needed.
- The ball should not be passed too hard during the 'take'.
- The player awaiting the ball should stand showing his team mate on which foot he would like to receive the pass.
- The player awaiting the ball should start moving towards the ball when the passer has recieved the ball.
- The supporting leg is often too far away from the ball and/or the player leans back.
- When passing the foot should be slightly lifted and swung downwards lightly towards the ball.
- Many players control and drivbble the ball with their 'laces'. Controlling the ball with the instep is much easier as a first step.

Field size:
12 x 12 m box

Cone margins:
Distance between the cones: 12 m

Materials:
4 cones

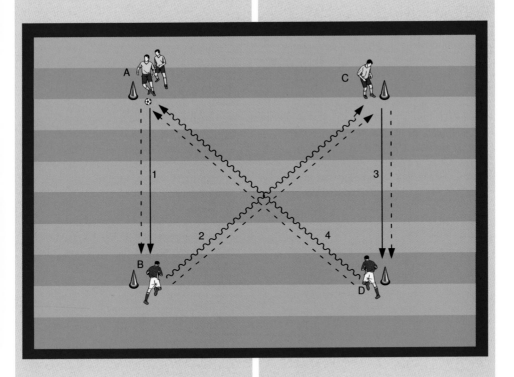

Training Target
- Ballskill (Touch on the ball)

Training Emphasis
- Passing
- Trapping

Training Aspects

Skills involved:	One touch passes, Passing in a square, Short passing
Age level:	9 years - Adult
Level of play:	Advanced
Type of training:	Group training
Training structure:	Progression, Main point/Emphasis
Purpose:	Improve individual skills
Total number of players:	6 players
Participating players:	Whole team
Training location:	Any
Spatial awareness:	Limited playing field
Duration:	10-20 min
Physiology:	Soccer-specific endurance, Power & Speed

Organization:
6 players take up their positions at the corners of the box. Two cones are occupied by three players. All of these players have a ball.

Process:
Players A + C (in possession) pass at the same time to B and D opposite and follow their passes. Players B and D pass diagonally and take up the positions from A & C. The vertical passes should be played and then the diagonal passes.

Tip:
The player should watch the whole field so as to not miss the next pass.
- The supporting foot should be 30-40cm to the side of the ball, in line with the ball.
- When passing with the instep, the toes should point upwards, the ankle joint should be tensed and the upper body slightly leant over the ball.
- Stand on the balls of your feet, the passing foot should be slightly raised to strike the ball in the middle. Bring your body over the ball and don't lean back. (Ball control is achieved using the same technique).
- The foot should follow through after striking the ball.
- Movement of the arms is important: When passing with the right instep the left arm should cross to the right hip; when passing with the left instep the right arm should cross to the left hip.
- The player can lean back slightly when passing with the outstep.
- When passing with the ball of the foot, the player approaches the ball diagonally with his body slightly to the side of the ball.

Field size:
12 x 12 m box

Cone margins:
Distance between the cones: 12 m

Materials:
4 cones

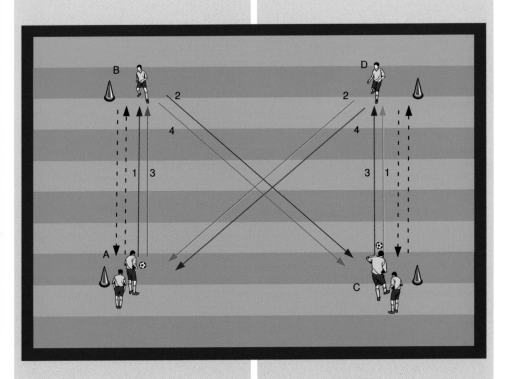

Training Target
- Ball skill (Touch on the ball)

Training Emphasis
- Passing

Training Aspects

Skills involved:	One touch passes, Passing in a square, Short passing
Age level:	9 years - Adult
Level of play:	Advanced
Type of training:	Group training
Training structure:	Warm-up, Progression, Main point/Emphasis
Purpose:	Improve individual skills
Total number of players:	8 players
Participating players:	Whole team
Training location:	Any
Spatial awareness:	Limited playing field
Duration:	10-15 min
Physiology:	Soccer-specific endurance, Power & Speed

Organization:
8 players take up their places in the box. Two players at every cone. Two players have a ball.

Process:
The players in possession start with their passes (see graphic). The players passing then run to take up the position of their teammates to the side. There is always a straight pass and then a diagonal pass. The positions should be changed as quickly as possible.

Tip:
The player should watch the whole field so as to not miss the next pass.
Further important characteristics:
- The supporting foot should be 30-40cm to the side of the ball, in line with the ball.
- When passing with the instep, the toes should point upwards, the ankle joint should be tensed and the upper body slightly leaning over the ball.

- Stand on the balls of your feet, the passing foot should be slightly raised to strike the ball in the middle. Bring your body over the ball and don't lean back. (Ball control is achieved using the same technique.)
- The foot should follow through after striking the ball.
- Movement of the arms is important: when passing with the right instep, the left arm should cross to the right hip; when passing with the left instep, the right arm should cross to the left hip.
- The player can lean back slightly when passing with the outstep.
- When passing with the ball of the foot, the player approaches the ball diagonally with his body slightly to the side of the ball.

Field size:
12 m box

Cone margins:
Distance between the cones: 12 m

Materials:
4 cones

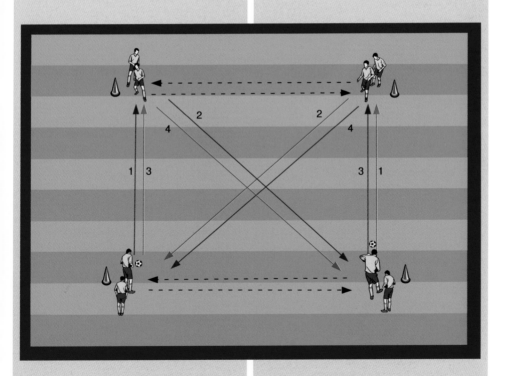

Training Target
- **Ballskill (Touch on the ball)**

Training Emphasis
- **Passing**
- **Trapping**

Training Aspects

Skills involved:	One touch passes, Wall passes, Controlling the ball
Age level:	9 years - Adult
Level of play:	Any, Advanced
Type of training:	Group training
Training structure:	Warm-up, Progression, Main point/Emphasis
Purpose:	Groups, Improve individual skills
Total number of players:	5 - 10 players
Participating players:	Whole team
Training location:	Any
Spatial awareness:	Limited playing field
Duration:	10-15 min
Physiology:	Soccer-specific endurance

Organization:
The diamond/cross is made up from 4 cones. Two players start at the large cones, 1 player at each of the small cones.

Process:
The blue player starts with a short pass to the blue player at the side who lays the ball off with his first touch. As soon as the ball has left the feet of the player laying the ball off, the first blue player follows his pass and passes directly to the red player stationed at the other large cone with his first touch. The red player then, with one touch, passes to the red player at the small cone on the other side who lays the ball off for him and the whole sequence runs again on the other side.

Alternative:
- After the first pass, the player laying the ball of can take one or two touches
- Everything one-touch with two balls.

Tip:
- The drill should, at first, be completed slowly and with one ball.
- The first passer of the ball must run towards the pass.
- Players usually run faster than they pass. This should be avoided.
- If the balls aren't passed hard enough or with enough precision then the drill breaks down.
- This drill requires a large amount of concentration.
- When controlling the ball, the player's supporting leg is often too far away from the ball, and/or the player leans back.
- Lots of player pass with their 'laces' or with the outstep. Passing and controlling with the instep is considerably easier as a first step.
- The player passing must should pass the ball diagonally on to the correct foot of his teammate so that he can pass/control the ball efficiently.

Field size:
Training area size 20 x 12 m

Cone margins:
Distance vertical (the distance between the
two cones which are occupied by 3
players): 20 m
Distance horizontal: 12 m

Materials:
4 cones

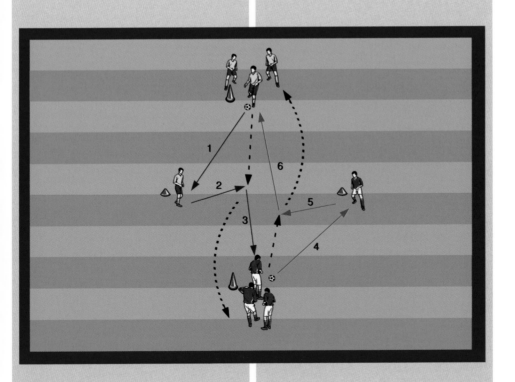

Training Target
- Ball skill (Touch on the ball)

Training Emphasis
- Passing

Training Aspects

Skills involved:	One touch passes, Passing in a rhombus, Short passing
Age level:	6 - 16 years
Level of play:	Any
Type of training:	Group training
Training structure:	Warm-up, Progression, Main point/Emphasis
Purpose:	Improve individual skills
Total number of players:	4 players
Participating players:	Whole team
Training location:	Any
Spatial awareness:	Limited playing field
Duration:	10-15 min

Organization:
Set up a diamond with cones, as shown. One player at each cone.

Process:
The blue and the red players pass the ball to one another, one-touch. As both pairs are passing at the same time, they have to make sure that the balls don't hit each other in the middle.

Tip:
Suitable pass speed, strength and precision.
- The supporting foot should be 30-40cm to the side of the ball, in line with the ball.
- When passing with the instep, the toes should point upwards, the ankle joint should be tensed and the upper body slightly leaning over the ball.
- Stand on the balls of your feet, the passing foot should be slightly raised to strike the ball in the middle. Bring your body over the ball and don't lean back. (Ball control is achieved using the same technique.)

- The foot should follow through after striking the ball.
- Movement of the arms is important: When passing with the right instep the left arm should cross to the right hip; when passing with the left instep the right arm should cross to the left hip.
- The player can lean back slightly when passing with the outstep.
- When passing with the ball of the foot, the player approaches the ball diagonally with his body slightly to the side of the ball.

Field size:
10 x 10 m square box

Cone margins:
Distance vertical/horizontal (opposing cones): 10 m

Materials:
4 cones

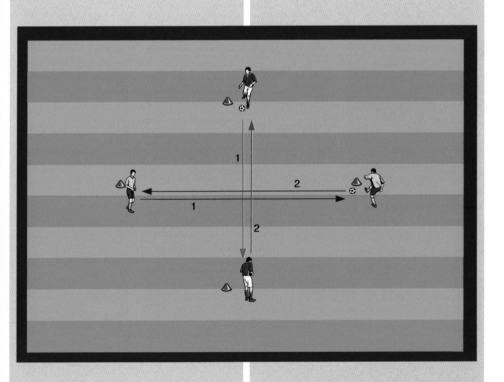

Training Target
- Ball skill (Touch on the ball)

Training Emphasis
- Passing

Training Aspects

Skills involved:	One touch passes, Wall passes, Passing over multiple stations
Age level:	9 years - Adult
Level of play:	Any
Type of training:	Group training
Training structure:	Warm-up, Progression, Main point/Emphasis
Purpose:	Groups, Improve individual skills
Total number of players:	8 players
Participating players:	Whole team
Training location:	Any
Spatial awareness:	Limited playing field
Duration:	10-15 min

Organization:
4 cones are laid out as shown. 3 players start at each of the large cones. One player starts at each of the small cones.

Process:
The blue player starts by passing to the blue player at the small cone who lays the ball off. The first blue player then passes with his first touch to the red player at the other small cone who also lays the ball back. The blue player then passes with his first touch to the players at the large cone at the other end of the drill. When the ball arrives, the same sequence continues from that end, starting with a one-two with the red player and then a one-two with the blue player. The blue player joins the red group after his two one-twos.

Tip:
- The player waiting for the ball starts moving towards the ball as the ball is passed.
- The player passing the ball must adjust his running speed to the speed of the ball.
- The supporting leg is often too far away from the ball and/or the player leans back.
- Timing of the pass is important.
- Players often run faster than they pass.
- Demand good strength of pass and pass precision.

Field size:
25 x 12 m

Cone margins:
The two large cones are 25 m apart. The small cones are 6 m to the side and 7 m behind the respective large cones.

Materials:
4 cones

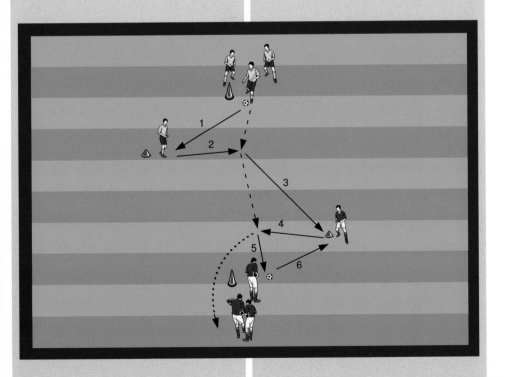

Training Target
- Ball skill (Touch on the ball)

Training Emphasis
- Passing

Training Aspects

Skills involved:	One touch passes
Age level:	9 years - Adult
Level of play:	Any
Type of training:	Group training
Training structure:	Progression, Main point/Emphasis
Purpose:	Groups, Improve individual skills
Total number of players:	6 players
Participating players:	Whole team
Training location:	Any
Spatial awareness:	Limited playing field
Duration:	10-15 min
Physiology:	Soccer-specific endurance, Power & Speed

Organization:
Two cones are set up opposing one another. Three players start at each cone. One group has a ball.

Process:
Each action is a double one-two.
Player A passes to player B who lays the ball off in space for A to run onto. Player A lays the ball off with his first touch into space for player B to run onto. B now passes over to the other side (the blue side). One-twos are then played from each side one after another.

Tip:
- The player waiting for the ball starts moving towards the ball as the ball is passed.
- The player passing the ball must adjust his running speed to the speed of the ball.
- The supporting leg is often too far away from the ball and/or the player leans back.
- Timing of the pass is important.
- Players often run faster than they pass.
- Demand good strength of pass and pass precision.

Field size:
25 x 12 m

Cone margins:
Distance between the 2 cones: 25 m

Materials:
2 cones

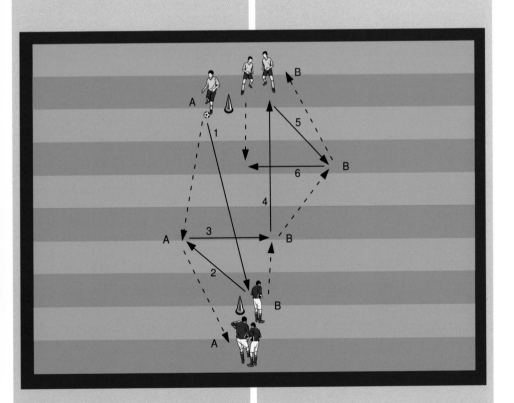

Training Target
- Ball skill (Touch on the ball)

Training Emphasis
- Passing

Training Aspects

Skills involved:	One touch passes, Wall passes, Passing over multiple stations
Age level:	9 years - Adult
Level of play:	Any
Type of training:	Group Training
Training structure:	Warm-up, Progression, Main point/Emphasis
Purpose:	Groups, Improve individual skills
Total number of players:	5 players
Participating players:	Whole team
Training location:	Any
Spatial awareness:	Limited playing field
Duration:	10-15 min
Physiology:	Soccer-specific endurance, Power & Speed

Organization:
Set up a box with cones, as shown. The starting poisition (the player with the ball) must be occupied by two players.

Process:
The sequence of passes is always the same. The player with the ball passes to the next player who comes to meet the ball. He then lays the ball back to the first player and runs around the cone from which he came and recieves the ball from A again. He then passes to the next player. Every player moves on to the next cone after their second pass.

Alternative:
The first pass should be one-touch, the player can then take two touches for the second pass.

Tip:
This drill will take time for the players to master.

- The player waiting for the ball starts moving towards the ball as the ball is passed.
- The player passing the ball must adjust his running speed to the speed of the ball.
- The supporting leg is often too far away from the ball and/or the player leans back.
- Timing of the pass is important.
- Players often run faster than they pass.
- Demand good strength of pass and pass precision.

Further important characteristics:
- The supporting foot should be 30-40cm to the side of the ball, in line with the ball.
- When passing with the instep, the toes should point upwards, the ankle joint should be tensed and the upper body slightly leant over the ball.
- Stand on the balls of your feet, the passing foot should be slightly raised to strike the ball in the middle. Bring your

body over the ball and don't lean back. (Ball control is achieved using the same technique).

- The foot should follow through after striking the ball.
- Movement of the arms is important: When passing with the right instep the left arm should cross to the right hip; when passing with the left instep the right arm should cross to the left hip.
- The player can lean back slightly when passing with the outstep.
- When passing with the ball of the foot, the player approaches the ball diagonally with his body slightly to the side of the ball.

Field size:
12 x 12 m

Cone margins:
Distance between the cones: 12 m

Materials:
4 cones

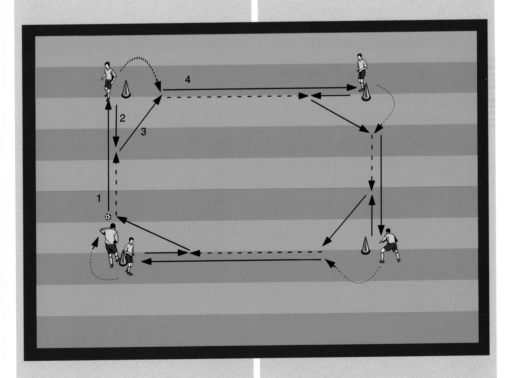

Training Target
- Ball skill (Touch on the ball)

Training Emphasis
- Passing

Training Aspects

Skills involved:	One touch passes, Wall passes, Passing over multiple stations
Age level:	9 years - Adult
Level of play:	Any
Type of training:	Group Training
Training structure:	Warm-up, Progression, Main point/Emphasis
Purpose:	Groups, Alone training
Total number of players:	6 players
Participating players:	Whole team
Training location:	Any
Spatial awareness:	Limited playing field
Duration:	10-20 min
Physiology:	Soccer-specific endurance

Organization:
Four cones make up a box. Two players stand at two of the cones and one at the other two.

Process:
The sequence of passes is always the same. The player with the ball passes to the next player who comes to meet the pass. He lays the ball back to the first player and then runs around the cone from where he came. The first player then passes diagonally to the next player who lays the ball off to the second player who has now encircled the cone. Every player moves on one cone after their second pass.

The drill can be done with two balls starting diagonally from each other at the same time. Those cones must be occupied by more than one player.

Tip:
- The player waiting for the ball starts moving towards the ball as the ball is passed.
- The player passing the ball must adjust his running speed to the speed of the ball.
- The supporting leg is often too far away from the ball and/or the player leans back.
- Timing of the pass is important.
- Players often run faster than they pass.
- Demand good strength of pass and pass precision.

Field size:
12 x 12 m

Cone margins:
Distance vertical/horizontal: 12 m

Materials:
4 cones

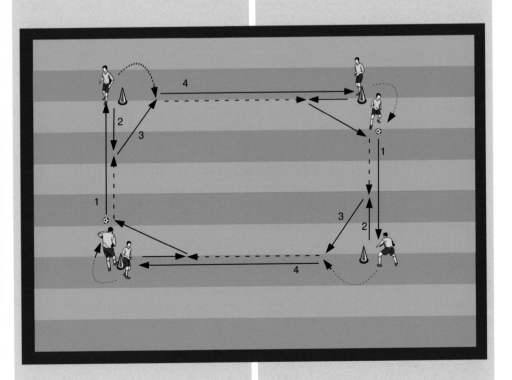

Training Target
- Ball skill (Touch on the ball)

Training Emphasis
- Passing

Training Aspects

Skills involved:	One touch passes, Wall passes, Passing over multiple stations
Age level:	9 years - Adult
Level of play:	Advanced, Professional
Type of training:	Group Training
Training structure:	Warm-up, Progression, Main point/Emphasis
Purpose:	Attack behavior, Groups, Improve individual skills
Total number of players:	5 players
Participating players:	Whole team
Training location:	Any
Spatial awareness:	Limited playing field
Duration:	10-15 min
Physiology:	Soccer-specific endurance, Power & Speed

Organization:
Set up a box with cones as shown. Two players must start at the starting position (where the ball is).

Process:
The player with the ball starts the passing sequence with pass (1) to the player in front of him. He then lays the ball back and runs around the cone. The first player then follows his pass and plays the return ball diagonally to the player top right. He lays the ball off to the second player who has now encircled the cone. He then passes the ball diagonally with his first touch to the player bottom right who lays the ball off to the player top right who has now also encircled his cone. Each player moves on one cone after their second pass. The passing sequence repeats itself continuously: Lay off, diagonal pass.

Tip:
- The player waiting for the ball starts moving towards the ball as the ball is passed.
- The player passing the ball must orientate his running speed to the speed of the ball.
- The supporting leg is often too far away from the ball and/or the player leans back.
- Timing of the pass is important.
- Players often run faster than they pass.
- Demand good strength of pass and pass precision.

Field size:
12 x 12 m box

Cone margins:
Distance between the cones: 12 m

Materials:
4 cones

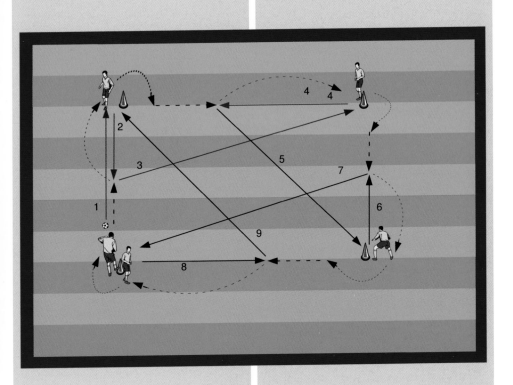

Training Target
- Ball skill (Touch on the ball)

Training Emphasis
- Passing

Training Aspects

Skills involved:	One touch passes, Wall passes, Passing over multiple stations, Passing in different formations
Age level:	Under 13 - Adult
Level of play:	Professional
Type of training:	Group training
Training structure:	Progression
Purpose:	Attack behavior, Stress training, Training for fun, Groups, Improve individual skills
Total number of players:	7 players
Participating players:	Whole team
Training location:	Any
Spatial awareness:	Limited playing field
Duration:	10-20 min
Physiology:	Soccer-specific endurance, Speed endurance, Power & Speed

Organization:
4 cones make up a box. Two players start at two of the cones, one player starts at each of the other cones. One player starts in the middle of the box.

Process:
6 players, 2 balls, player in the middle.
The passing sequence takes place with at least 5 players and two balls simultaneously, 7 players is ideal. The players with the ball have lots of options and can decide where they pass to. The player in the middle can be used to play a one-two although he can decide for himself where he passes the ball on to. All the cones must always be taken up by at least one player. Each player can also decide, based on the situation, to which cone he runs. When possible, the player should run to a cone different from the one to which he has passed.

Tip:
- The focus is on quick, ever-changing, creative passing and movement.
- This drill requires a large amount of concentration and improves game intelligence.
- There are always lots of new options.
- Anticipation, awareness, reaction and speed of thought and movement are trained intensively here.

Field size:
12 x 12 m box

Cone margins:
Distance vertical/horizontal: 12 m

Materials:
4 cones

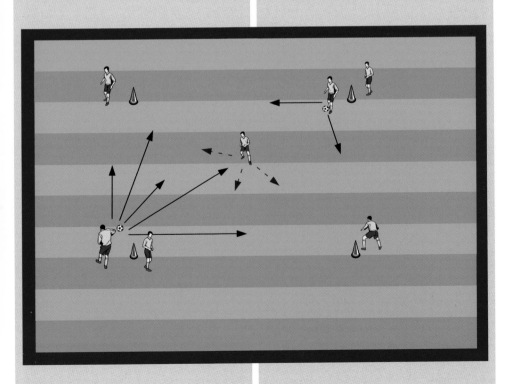

Training Target
- Ball skill (Touch on the ball)

Training Emphasis
- Passing

Training Aspects

Skills involved:	One touch passes, Wall passes, Passing over multiple stations, Passing in different formations, Short passing
Age level:	15 years - Adult
Level of play:	Professional
Type of training:	Group training
Training structure:	Progression, Main point/Emphasis
Purpose:	Attack behavior, Groups, Improve individual skills
Total number of players:	7 players
Participating players:	Whole team
Training location:	Any
Spatial awareness:	Limited playing field
Duration:	10-20 min
Physiology:	Soccer-specific endurance, Power & Speed

Organization:
6 cones are laid out as shown. Two players start at the start position, one player at each of the other cones.

Process:
The passing sequence starts with a one-two between A and B and then continues with a cross-field pass to C. C lays the ball off for B to run on to and moves immediately after his pass towards B to the side. C then passes to D. B takes up the position from C, C the position from D and A the positions from B. The same sequence then continues on the opposite side.

Tip:
- Precise, exact passing is extremely important for successful soccer. As a result passing should be regularly practiced. It is important not to forget to correct mistakes and give correct demonstrations.

Further important characteristics:
- The supporting foot should be 30-40cm to the side of the ball, in line with the ball.
- When passing with the instep, the toes should point upwards, the ankle joint should be tensed and the upper body slightly leant over the ball.
- Stand on the balls of your feet, the passing foot should be slightly raised to strike the ball in the middle. Bring your body over the ball and don't lean back. (Ball control is achieved using the same technique).
- The foot should follow through after striking the ball.
- Movement of the arms is important: When passing with the right instep the left arm should cross to the right hip; when passing with the left instep the right arm should cross to the left hip.
- The player can lean back slightly when passing with the outstep.

- When passing with the ball of the foot, the player approaches the ball diagonally with his body slightly to the side of the ball.

Materials:
6 cones

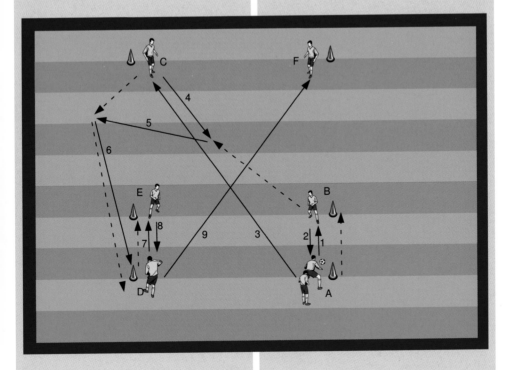

Training Target
- Ball skill (Touch on the ball)

Training Emphasis
- Passing
- Trapping

Training Aspects

Skills involved:	One touch passes, Passing over multiple stations, Short passing, Dribbling
Age level:	9 years - Adult
Level of play:	Any
Type of training:	Group training
Training structure:	Warm-up, Progression, Main point/Emphasis
Purpose:	Attack behavior, Groups, Improve individual skills
Total number of players:	5 players
Participating players:	Whole team
Training location:	Any
Spatial awareness:	Limited playing field
Duration:	10-20 min
Physiology:	Soccer-specific endurance, Speed endurance, Power & Speed

Organization:
8 cones are laid out as shown. The cone with two players is the starting position.

Process:
Player A starts by passing the ball through the cone goal. Player B turns with the ball and dribbles at speed to the next cone. B then plays a short pass to C. A takes up the position of B and B goes between the cone goal.

The same passing sequence then continues (C + D).

Tip:
- The player waiting for the ball starts moving towards the ball as the ball is passed.
- The player passing the ball must adjust his running speed to the speed of the ball.
- The supporting leg is often too far away from the ball and/or the player leans back.
- Timing of the pass is important.
- Players often run faster than they pass.
- Demand good strength of pass and pass precision.
- Good speed dribbling with short steps. The ball shouldn't be farther than 50cm away from the foot.

Field size:
15 x 15 m box

Cone margins:
Distance corner cones: 15 m
Distance middle cone: 7.5 m
Size of cone goals: 2 m

Materials:
8 cones

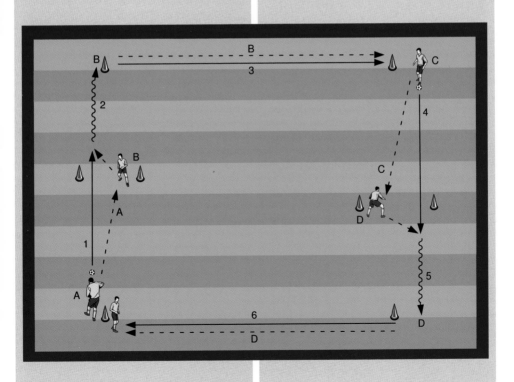

Training Target
• Ballskill (Touch on the ball)

Training Emphasis
• Passing

Training Aspects

Skills involved:	One touch passes, Control
Age level:	9 years - Adult
Level of play:	Any, Advanced
Type of training:	Group Training
Training structure:	Warm-up, Progression
Purpose:	Attack behavior, Groups, Improve individual skills
Total number of players:	10 players, 9 players
Participating players:	Whole team
Training location:	Any
Spatial awareness:	Limited playing field
Duration:	10-20 min
Physiology:	Soccer-specific endurance, Speed endurance, Power & Speed

Organization:
Two boxes, one large and one small. A player starts at each cone. The start cone has two players and the ball.

Process:
The passing starts with a diagonal ball. The receiver lays the ball off to the player opposite to him. This player passes the ball out of the inner box. These three variations are continuously repeated. Each player follows his pass and joins the cone to which he passed.

Alternative:
Start with maximum 3 touches, then two, then one.
When the drill is flowing, a second ball can be introduced. Start at the same time at cones A + B. 10 players are necessary in this variation because of the 2 balls. Two players start at each of the start cones (i.e. A + B). Now the players have to concentrate on the other ball in order to keep the rhythm and the distance between the balls the same.

Tip:
• When the drill is done with two touches, (control + pass) attention needs to be paid to the position of the foot and should be corrected accordingly.
• The receiver should make a dynamic dummy run away from the player before receiving the pass.
• Strong, precise passes on the ground.
• The foot should be slightly lifted when laying the ball off.

Field size:
Outer box: 24 x 24 m

Cone margins:
The outer cones are 24 m apart. The inner cones are 6 m away. The distance between the cones in the inner box is 11 m.

Materials:
8 cones

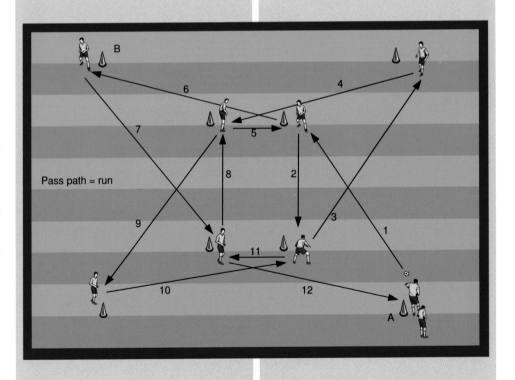

Pass path = run

Training Target
- Ball skill (Touch on the ball)

Training Emphasis
- Passing

Training Aspects

Skills involved:	One touch passes, Wall passes, Passing over multiple stations
Age level:	Under 15 - Adult
Level of play:	Beginner
Type of training:	Group Training
Training structure:	Warm-up, Progression, Main point/Emphasis
Purpose:	Attack behavior, Groups, Improve individual skills
Total number of players:	9 players
Participating players:	Whole team
Training location:	Any
Spatial awareness:	Limited playing field
Duration:	10-20 min
Physiology:	Soccer-specific endurance, Power & Speed

Organization:
There is a large box and a small box. One player starts at each cone. There are two players at the start cone.

Process:
Player A passes up to B who plays a one-two with H (past player G). B then passes up to C who plays a one-two with G, etc. Players A, B, C, and D move on one position after their passes. Players E, F, G and H now complete the same sequence of passes and moves. They run towards the passer, move the ball on past the player at the cone and move on to the next position. The same sequence always flows in the same direction.

Tip:
- The players should try to give the passer a signal (call for the ball)
- The player waiting for the ball starts moving towards the ball as the ball is passed.
- The player passing the ball must orientate his running speed to the speed of the ball.
- The supporting leg is often too far away from the ball and/or the player leans back.
- Timing of the pass is important.
- Players often run faster than they pass.
- Demand good strength of pass and pass precision.

Field size:
24 x 24 m box

Cone margins:
Outer box: 24 m
Inner box: 12 m

Materials:
8 cones

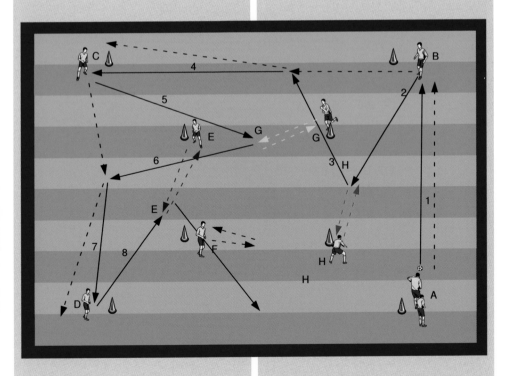

Training Target
- Ball skill (Touch on the ball)

Training Emphasis
- Passing

Training Aspects

Skills involved:	One touch passes, Passing over multiple stations, Short passing
Age level:	9 years - Adult
Level of play:	Any
Type of training:	Group training
Training structure:	Warm-up, Progression, Main point/Emphasis
Purpose:	Attack behavior, Groups, Improve individual skills
Total number of players:	8 players
Participating players:	Whole team
Training location:	Any
Spatial awareness:	Limited playing field
Duration:	10-20 min
Physiology:	Soccer-specific endurance, Speed endurance, Power & Speed

Organization:
A large box and a small box are formed with 8 cones. One player starts at each cone. The player at the start position has a ball.

Process:
The sequence is started with a pass to the first inner cone. This player passes with his first touch to the outer cone. This combination repeats itself continuously. The players change position, as shown, horizontally, irrespective of whether they are in the outside box or the inside box.

Alternative:
After a few minutes the players change positions from the inner to the outer box.

Tip:
- This drill is very tiring.
- The supporting leg is often too far away from the ball and/or the player leans back.
- Timing of the pass is important.
- Players often run faster than they pass.
- Demand good strength of pass and pass precision.

Field size:
20 x 20 m

Cone margins:
The outer cones are 20 m apart. The inner cones 10. The distance between the inner box and the next cone is 5 m.

Materials:
8 cones

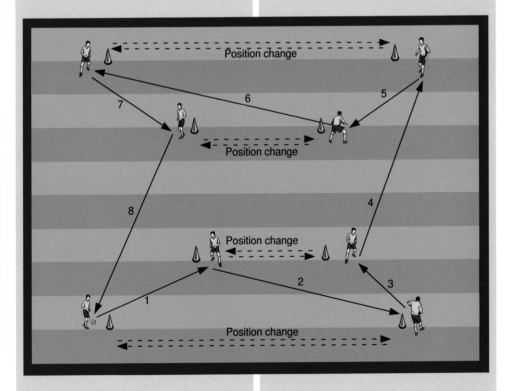

Training Target
- Ball skill (Touch on the ball)

Training Emphasis
- Passing

Training Aspects

Skills involved:	One touch passes, Passing over multiple stations, Short passing
Age level:	9 years - Adult
Level of play:	Any
Type of training:	Group training
Training structure:	Progression, Main point/Emphasis
Purpose:	Attack behavior, Groups, Improve individual skills
Total number of players:	8 players
Participating players:	Whole team
Training location:	Any
Spatial awareness:	Limited playing field
Duration:	10-20 min
Physiology:	Soccer-specific endurance, Speed endurance, Power & Speed

Organization:
A large box and a small box are formed with 8 cones. One player starts at each cone. The player at the start position has a ball.

Process:
The first pass is square (horizontal) (1) followed by 2 diagonal, cross-field passes (inwards 2 and outwards 3). The same passing sequence is required contiuously. The players change places vertically, irrespective of whether they are in the inner or outer box.

Alternative:
After a few minutes the players change positions from the inner to the outer box.

Tip:
- This drill is very tiring.
- The supporting leg is often too far away from the ball and/or the player leans back.
- Timing of the pass is important.
- Players often run faster than they pass.
- Demand good strength of pass and pass precision.

Field size:
20 x 20 m

Cone margins:
The outer cones are 20 m apart. The inner cones 10. The distance between the inner box and the next cone is 5m.

Materials:
8 cones

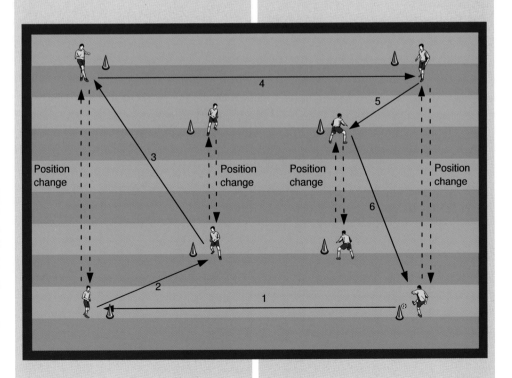

Training Target
- Ball skill (Touch on the ball)

Training Emphasis
- Passing

Training Aspects

Skills involved:	One touch passes, Passing over multiple stations, Short passing
Age level:	9 years - Adult
Level of play:	Beginner
Type of training:	Group Training
Training structure:	Progression, Main point/Emphasis
Purpose:	Groups, Improve individual skills
Total number of players:	10 players
Participating players:	Whole team
Training location:	Any
Spatial awareness:	Limited playing field
Duration:	10-20 min
Physiology:	Soccer-specific endurance, Power & Speed

Organization:
A large box and a small box are formed with 8 cones. 10 players occupy the cones. The two start cones should be occupied by more than one player.

Process:
The drill starts with a square ball from both players at the start positions to their neighbors (1). This is followed by two cross-field passes. The first pass is passed from the player in the outer box to the player closest to him in the inner box. The second pass is passed to the next player in the outer box (2+3). After each pass players change places horizontally so that the positions are permanently changed, this way there is always movement in the game.

Alterrnative:
After a few minutes the players change positions from the inner to the outer box.

Tip:
- This drill is very tiring.
- The supporting leg is often too far away from the ball and/or the player leans back.
- Timing of the pass is important.
- Players often run faster than they pass.
- Demand good strength of pass and pass precision.

Field size:
20 x 20 m

Cone margins:
cones outer box: 20 m
cones inner box: 10 m

Materials:
8 cones

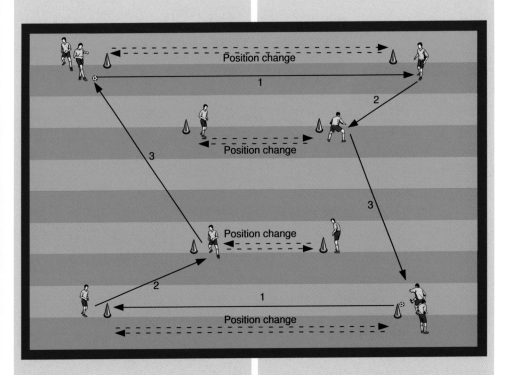

Training Target
- Ball skill (Touch on the ball)

Training Emphasis
- Passing

Training Aspects

Skills involved:	One touch passes, Passing over multiple stations, Passing in a triangle, Short passing
Age level:	9 years - Adult
Level of play:	Any
Type of training:	Group training
Training structure:	Progression, Main point/Emphasis
Purpose:	Attack behavior, Groups, Improve individual skills
Total number of players:	8 players
Participating players:	Whole team
Training location:	Any
Spatial awareness:	Limited playing field
Duration:	10-20 min
Physiology:	Soccer-specific endurance, Speed endurance, Power & Speed

Organization:

A large box and a small box are formed with 8 cones. 6 players spread themselves across the cones as shown. Two players start at the first cones. Each group of four has one ball.

Process:

The first pass is a vertical pass (1) to player B, followed by a pass for C to run on to. Player C passes back to the start to player D. The 3 players on the other side of the drill, run the exercise at the same time.

Tip:
- This drill is very tiring.
- The supporting leg is often too far away from the ball and/or the player leans back.
- Timing of the pass is important.
- Players often run faster than they pass.
- Demand good strength of pass and pass precision.
- Pass precision is more important than pass speed.
- The second pass must be passed for player to run on to.

Field size:
20 x 20 m

Cone margins:
The outer cones are 20m apart. The inner cones 10. The distance between the inner box and the next cone is 5 m.

Materials:
8 cones

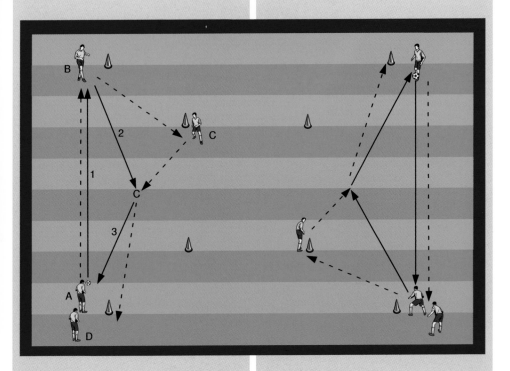

Training Target
- Ball skill (Touch on the ball)

Training Emphasis
- Passing

Training Aspects

Skills involved:	One touch passes, Passing over multiple stations, Short passing
Age level:	9 years - Adult
Level of play:	Advanced
Type of training:	Group training
Training structure:	Progression, Main point/Emphasis
Purpose:	Attack behavior, Groups, Improve individual skills
Total number of players:	10 or more players
Participating players:	Whole team
Training location:	Any
Spatial awareness:	Limited playing field
Duration:	10-20 min
Physiology:	Soccer-specific endurance, Speed endurance, Power & Speed

Organization:
A large box and a small box are formed with 8 cones. 16 players spread themselves across the cones as shown. Two players start at the first cones. Each group of four has one ball.

Process:
The drill starts with a long ball (1 - vertical) from A to B follwoed by a pass for C to run on to. Player C then passes the ball back to the start position to player D. This exercise can continue at the same time with 4 players per drill at the other 3 sets of cones.

Tip:
- This drill is very tiring.
- The supporting leg is often too far away from the ball and/or the player leans back.
- Timing of the pass is important.
- Players often run faster than they pass.
- Demand good strength of pass and pass precision.
- Pass precision is more important than pass speed.
- The second pass must be passed for player to run on to.

Field size:
20 x 20 m

Cone margins:
The outer cones are 20 m apart. The inner cones 10. The distance between the inner box and the next cone is 5m.

Materials:
8 cones

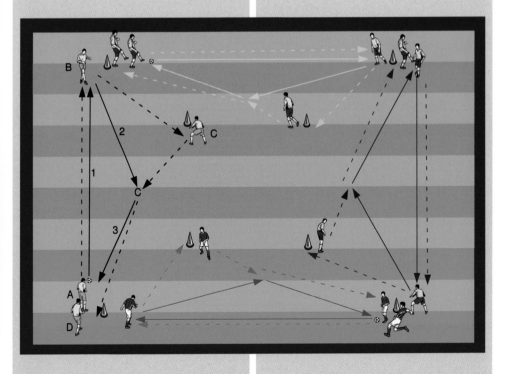

Training Target
- Ball skill (Touch on the ball)

Training Emphasis
- Passing

Training Aspects

Skills involved:	One touch passes, Passing over multiple stations, Passing in different formations, Short passing
Age level:	13 years - Adult
Level of play:	Advanced, Professional
Type of training:	Group training
Training structure:	Warm-up, Progression, Main point/Emphasis
Purpose:	Attack behavior, Groups, Improve individual skills
Total number of players:	7 players
Participating players:	Whole team
Training location:	Any
Spatial awareness:	Limited playing field
Duration:	10-20 min
Physiology:	Soccer-specific endurance, Speed endurance, Power & Speed

Organization:
Two triangles are set up next to one another. A players starts at each cone. Two players start at the start position.

Process:
Player D starts with a cross-field pass to A and then runs to cone VI. Player A plays a one-two with B and takes up his position at cone IV. B runs to cone V. Player C passes the ball (5) on to player F and runs to cone III. F then plays a one-two with D. The sequence of passes and runs continuously repeats itself so that in the process every player takes up every position.

Tip:
- This drill is very tiring and requires a great deal of player intelligence.
- The supporting leg is often too far away from the ball and/or the player leans back.
- Timing of the pass is important.
- Don't forget the runs.
- Demand good strength of pass and pass precision.
- Pass precision is more important than pass speed.
- Concentration must be held at all times.
- Anticipation, awareness, reaction, speed of thought and movement with and without the ball are continuously required.

Field size:
20 x 20 m

Cone margins:
The outer cones are 20 m apart. The inner cones 10. The distance between the inner box and the next cone is 5 m.

Materials:
6 cones

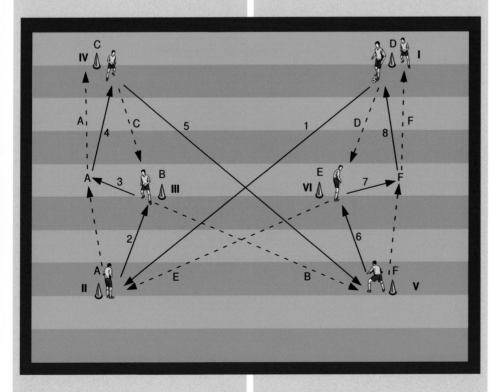

Training Target
- Ball skill (Touch on the ball)

Training Emphasis
- Passing

Training Aspects

Skills involved:	One touch passes, Wall passes, Passing over multiple stations, Passing in a square, Short passing
Age level:	Under 12 - Adult
Level of play:	Any
Type of training:	Group training
Training structure:	Warm-up, Progression, Main point/Emphasis
Purpose:	Attack behavior, Groups, Improve individual skills
Total number of players:	10 players, 8 players
Participating players:	Whole team
Training location:	Any
Spatial awareness:	Limited playing field
Duration:	10-20 min
Physiology:	Soccer-specific endurance, Speed endurance, Power & Speed

Organization:
A box is required. One player starts at each box, three players start at the start cone. The ball is with the group of 3.

Process:
The drill starts at the cone with three players. A pass is played to the receiver who comes towards the ball (1). The teammate then lays off the ball (2). The starting player passes the ball cross-field to the next player (3) etc.

In principle: long ball - lay off - cross-field ball

The passer and player laying off the ball swap positions. The sequence repeats itself continuously.

Alternative:
The drill can start with 2 balls at the same time. Both diagonally opposite positions must have at least 2 players.

Tip:
- Timing of the pass is important.
- Don't forget the runs.
- Demand good strength of pass and pass precision.
- Pass precision is more important than pass speed.
- Concentration must be held at all times.
- Anticipation, awareness, reaction, speed of thought and movement with and without the ball are continuously

Field size:
15 x 15 m

Cone margins:
Distance horizontal/vertical: 15 m

Materials:
4 cones

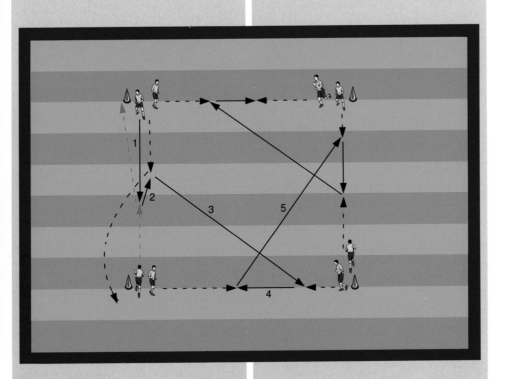

Training Target
- Ball skill (Touch on the ball)

Training Emphasis
- Passing

Training Aspects

Skills involved:	One touch passes, Wall passes, Passing over multiple stations, Passing in a square, Short passing
Age level:	13 years - Adult
Level of play:	Advanced
Type of training:	Group training
Training structure:	Warm-up, Progression, Main point/Emphasis
Purpose:	Attack behavior, Groups, Improve individual skills
Total number of players:	7 players
Participating players:	Whole team
Training location:	Any
Spatial awareness:	Limited playing field
Duration:	10-20 min
Physiology:	Soccer-specific endurance, Speed endurance, Power & Speed

Organization:
6 cones are laid out as shown, i.e. 4 cones make up the outer box in which 2 further cones are placed. One player per cone. The start cone must have 2 players.

Process:
The drill starts at the cone with 2 players. The first pass is in the middle, where the ball is laid off (2). Then the ball is passed cross-field (3). After that the player passes a square ball (4). The same sequence now takes place in the opposite direction (5-8).

The 4 outer players follow their passes. The two players in the middle move diagonally after their pass to the outer cone (red dotted line).

Tip:
- This drill is very tiring and requires a great deal of player intelligence.
- The supporting leg is often too far away from the ball and/or the player leans back.
- Timing of the pass is important.
- Don't forget the runs.
- Demand good strength of pass and pass precision.
- Pass precision is more important than pass speed.
- Concentratuion must be held at all times.
- Anticipation, awareness, reaction, speed of thought and movement with and without the ball are continuously required.

Field size:
15 x 15 m

Cone margins:
The two outer cones are 15 m apart. The third cone is central at a distance of 7.5 m from the outer cones and set off at a distance of 6 m.

Materials:
6 cones

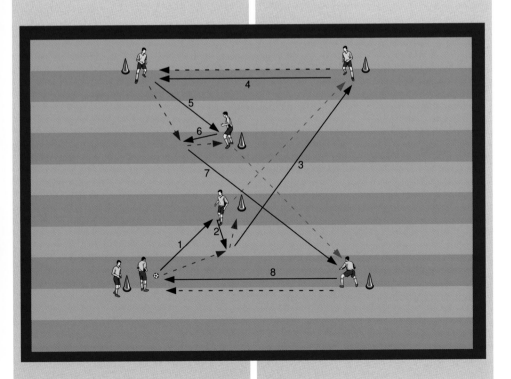

Training Target
- Ball skill (Touch on the ball)

Training Emphasis
- Passing

Training Aspects

Skills involved:	One touch passes, Wall passes, Passing over multiple stations, Short passing
Age level:	9 years - Adult
Level of play:	Advanced
Type of training:	Group training
Training structure:	Warm-up, Progression, Main point/Emphasis
Purpose:	Attack behavior, Groups, Improve individual skills
Total number of players:	10 players
Participating players:	Whole team
Training location:	Any
Spatial awareness:	Limited playing field
Duration:	10-20 min
Physiology:	Soccer-specific endurance, Speed endurance, Power & Speed

Organization:
6 cones are laid out as shown, i.e. 4 cones make up the outer box in which 2 further cones are placed. One player per cone. The start cone must have 2 players.

Process:
The drill starts simultaneously at the two cones where three players are standing. The first pass is into the middle (1) where the ball is laid off (2). After that a cross-field pass is played (3). The next pass is a square pass (4). The same sequence now takes place in the opposite direction.

The 4 outer players follow their passes. The two players in the middle move diagonally after their pass to the outer cone (red dotted line).

Tip:
- This drill is very tiring and requires a great deal of player intelligence.
- The supporting leg is often too far away from the ball and/or the player leans back.
- Timing of the pass is important.
- Don't forget the runs.
- Demand good strength of pass and pass precision.
- Pass precision is more important than pass speed.
- Concentratuion must be held at all times.
- Anticipation, awareness, reaction, speed of thought and movement with and without the ball are continuously required.
- The drills should run simultaneously. As a result the players must communicate and keep an eye on the other drill.

Field size:
15 x 15 m

Cone margins:
The two outer cones are 15 m apart. The third cone is central at a distance of 7.5 m from the outer cones and set off at a distance of 6 m.

Materials:
6 cones

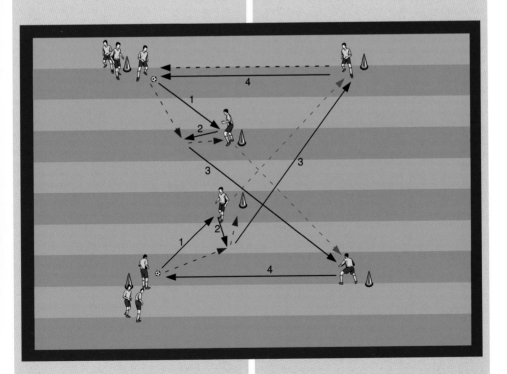

Training Target
- Ballskill (Touch on the ball)

Training Emphasis
- Passing

Training Aspects

Skills involved:	Passing over multiple stations, Passing in different formations, Passing in a square, Short passing, Long passing
Age level:	13 years - Adult
Level of play:	Advanced
Type of training:	Group training
Training structure:	Warm-up, Progression, Main point/Emphasis
Purpose:	Attack behavior, Groups, Improve individual skills
Total number of players:	8 players
Participating players:	Whole team
Training location:	Any
Spatial awareness:	Limited playing field
Duration:	10-20 min
Physiology:	Soccer-specific endurance, Speed endurance, Power & Speed

Process:
The players play in pairs:
(A+A) - red team
(B+B) - yellow team
(C+C) - blue team
(D+D) - grey team

The two pairs in possession must play at least three passes before they are allowed to pass the ball to the players in zone 3. The third pair tries to intercept the ball through clever pressing and energetic tackling. If they manage this, then they swap positions with the pair which lost the ball. After the third successful uninterrupted pass, if possible, the pair should pass the ball into the other zone to D+D. The pair which played the pass sprints, closely followed by the defensive pair, after the ball and continues the drill in the other zone. The defenders remain in their positions until they have intercepted the ball or for a maximum of 2 minutes.

Alternative:
- no restrictions on touches
- Restricted touches (e.g. 1-3 touches)

Tip:
- This drill is very tiring and requires a great deal of player intelligence.
- Good touch and combination soccer is required.
- The supporting leg is often too far away from the ball and/or the player leans back.
- Demand good strength of pass and pass precision.
- Pass precision is more important than pass speed.
- Concentratuion must be held at all times.
- Anticipation, awareness, reaction, speed of thought and movement with and without the ball are continuously required.
- The aims of this drill are switching from offense to defense, crossing the middle zone quickly and the setting up of new passing situations.

Field size:
35 x 10 m

Cone margins:
The outer zones are 10 x 10 m. The distance between the cones in the inner zone is 15 m horizontally and 10m vertically.

Materials:
8 cones

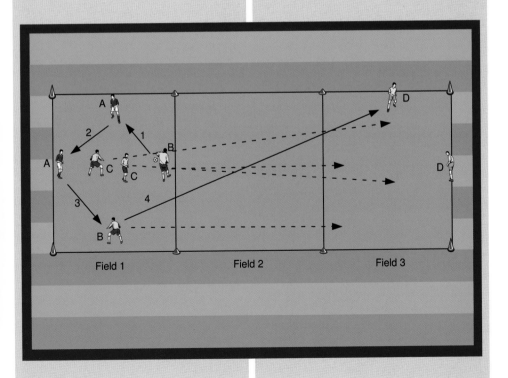

Field 1   Field 2   Field 3

Training Target
- Ball skill (Touch on the ball)

Training Emphasis
- Passing

Training Aspects

Skills involved:	Passing over multiple stations, Passing in a square, Short passing, Long passing, Combining technical skill with movement
Age level:	13 years - Adult
Level of play:	Advanced
Type of training:	Group Training
Training structure:	Warm-up, Progression, Main point/Emphasis
Purpose:	Groups, Improve individual skills
Total number of players:	10 players
Participating players:	Whole team
Training location:	Any
Spatial awareness:	Limited playing field
Duration:	10-20 min
Physiology:	Soccer-specific endurance

Organization:
Using 8 cones, three zones are marked out next to each other. The three zones make up the whole field of play (marked light green). Each of the boxes is labelled zone 1, 2 or 3. The zone with the ball is filled with 6 players. The middle zone (zone 2) has 2 players. Zone 3 also has 2 players.

Process:
The players play in pairs:
(A+A) - red team
(B+B) - yellow team
(C+C) - blue team
(D+D) - grey team
(E+E) - blue team

The two pairs in possession must play at least three passes before they are allowed to pass the ball to the players in zone 2. The third pair tries to intercept the ball through clever pressing and energetic tackling. If they manage this, then they swap positions with the pair which lost the ball. After the third successful uninterupted pass, if possible, the pair should pass the ball into zone 2. The players in zone 2 must both touch the ball before passing into zone 3. The player who passed the ball follows his pass together with his partner and the two defenders (C+C). The drill is then repeated with (E+E) together.

The defenders remain in their positions until they have intercepted the ball, the ball is played out or for a maximum of 2 minutes.

Alternative:
- no restrictions on touches
- Restricted touches (e.g. 1-3 touches)

Tip:
- This drill is very tiring and requires a great deal of player intelligence.
- Good touch and combination soccer is required.
- The supporting leg is often too far away from the ball and/or the player leans back.
- Demand good strength of pass and pass precision.

- Pass precision is more important than pass speed.
- Concentration must be held at all times.
- Anticipation, awareness, reaction, speed of thought and movement with and without the ball are continuously required.
- The zones in which the players compete change regularly, so creating a new game situation each time.

Field size:
35 x 10 m

Materials:
8 cones

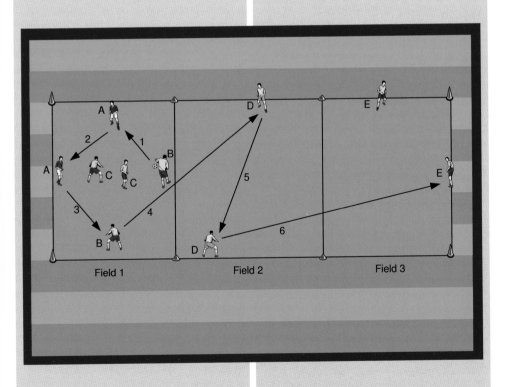

Field 1   Field 2   Field 3

Training Target
- **Ball skill (Touch on the ball)**

Training Emphasis
- **Passing**

Training Aspects

Skills involved:	One touch passes, Wall passes, Passing over multiple stations, Passing in a triangle, Short passing, Long passing
Age level:	Under 12 - Adult
Level of play:	Advanced, Professional
Type of training:	Group training
Training structure:	Warm-up, Progression, Main point/Emphasis
Purpose:	Attack behavior, Groups, Improve individual skills
Total number of players:	4-6 players
Participating players:	Whole team
Training location:	Any
Spatial awareness:	Limited playing field
Duration:	10-15 min
Physiology:	Soccer-specific endurance, Speed endurance, Strength endurance, Power & Speed

Organization:
Three cones are set up as shown. More than one player starts at the first cone. The ball is at the first cone. Each other player stands at one cone.

Process:
A plays a one-two with player B (1+2) and then passes cross-field to player C (3). C then plays a one-two with B (4+5) and passes the ball cross-field to cone II (i.e. Player A, who has now taken up his position there.) The same sequence now starts from the beginning again.

Runs:
- Player A runs to cone II
- B runs to cone III
- C runs to cone I
The positions are changed clockwise.

Alternative:
After half the time, the direction of play can be changed, i.e. the sequence runs counter-clockwise.

Tip:
Start by running the drill slowly and then speed up. The receiver should always make a small, dynamic dummy run away from the ball before receiving the ball. The drill can be extremely tiring when conducted quickly with only 4 players.
- Under time pressure, this drill is very game realistic.
- The receiver should call for the ball.
- Pass and run timing is important.
- Players often run faster than their pass.
- Don't forget the runs.
- Demand good strength of pass and pass precision.
- Pass precision is more important than pass speed.
- Concentration must be held at all times.

Field size:
12 x 12 m

Cone margins:
Distance between the cones: 12 m

Materials:
3 cones

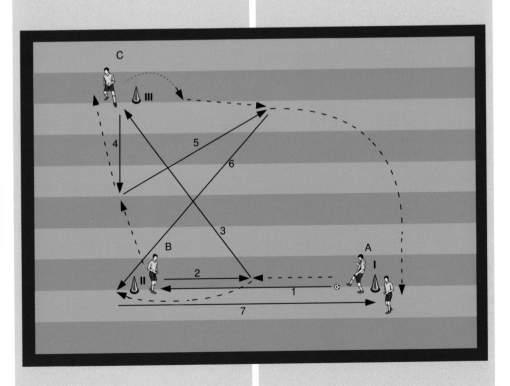

Training Target
- **Ball skill (Touch on the ball)**

Training Emphasis
- **Passing**

Training Aspects

Skills involved:	One touch passes, Wall passes, Passing over multiple stations, Passing in a triangle, Short passing, Long passing
Age level:	Under 12 - Adult
Level of play:	Advanced, Professional
Type of training:	Group training
Training structure:	Warm-up, Progression, Main point/Emphasis
Purpose:	Attack behavior, Groups, Improve individual skills
Total number of players:	4-6 players
Participating players:	Whole team
Training location:	Any
Spatial awareness:	Limited playing field
Duration:	10-15 min
Physiology:	Soccer-specific endurance, Speed endurance, Power & Speed

Organization:
Three cones are set up as shown. More than one player starts at the first cone. The ball is at the first cone. Every other player stands at one cone.

Process:
A plays a one-two with player B (1+2) and then passes cross-field to player C (3). C then plays a one-two with B (4+5) and then C plays a further one-two with D (6+7). After that player C (8) passes cross-field to cone II (i.e. Player A, who has now taken up his position there). Player A passes the ball to D (9). The same sequence now starts again.

Runs:
- Player A runs to cone II
- B runs to cone III
- C runs to cone I
The positions are changed clockwise.

Alternative:
After half the time, the direction of play can be changed, i.e. the sequence runs anti-clockwise.

Tip:
Start by running the drill slowly and then speed up. The receiver should always make a small, dynamic dummy run away from the ball before receiving the ball. The drill can be extremely tiring when conducted quickly with only 4 players.
- Under time pressure, this drill is very game realistic.
- The reciever should call for the ball.
- Pass and run timing is important
- Players often run faster than their pass.
- Don't forget the runs.
- Demand good strength of pass and pass precision.
- Pass precision is more important than pass speed.
- Concentration must be held at all times.

Field size:
12 X 12 m

Cone margins:
Distance between the cones: 12 m

Materials:
3 cones

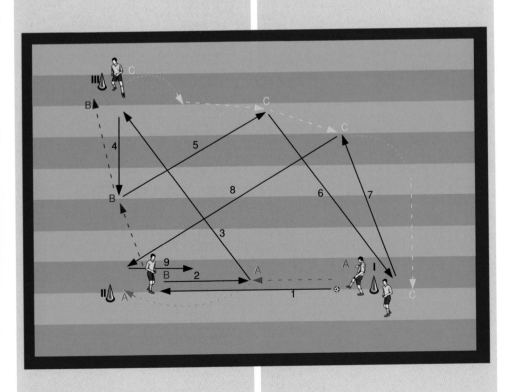

Training Target
- Ball skill (Touch on the ball)

Training Emphasis
- Passing

Training Aspects

Skills involved:	One touch passes, Wall passes, Passing in a triangle
Age level:	13 years - Adult
Level of play:	Advanced
Type of training:	Group Training
Training structure:	Warm-up, Progression, Main point/Emphasis
Purpose:	Groups, Improve individual skills
Total number of players:	7 players
Participating players:	Whole team
Training location:	Any
Spatial awareness:	Limited playing field
Duration:	10-20 min
Physiology:	Soccer-specific endurance, Speed endurance, Power & Speed

Organization:
Make 3 triangles using 9 cones (see graphic). Three players start at the starting cone of each triangle. 2 players start at each of the other cones.

Process:
Player A starts the drill by passing on the ground to B. He, having made a short, dynamic dummy move away from the ball before receiving it, lays the ball back to A who has followed his pass. When B lays off the ball, C begins his dummy run away from the ball. The following moves take place simultaneously: C leaves his starting position and sprints towards D. Player A passes the laid off ball from B in space for C to run onto who then passes on to D. Player B at the same time sprints to the start postion of C and takes over his former position. A takes up the position of B. This cycle remains the same and, ideally, should remain the same until the end of the drill.

The pass sequence is always: long ball, lay off, vertical pass. The order of the runs is always the same. The passer (of the long ball) runs (after the one-two) vertically onto the next cone. The player, who lays the ball off, runs around the triangle.

Tip:
Start by running the drill slowly and then speed up. The receiver should always make a small, dynamic dummy run away from the ball before receiving the ball. The drill can be extremely tiring when conducted quickly with only 7 players.
- This can be a very challenging passing drill, due to the large amount of running.
- Under time pressure, this drill is very game realistic.
- The reciever should call for the ball.
- Pass and run timing is important
- Players often run faster than their pass.
- Pass precision is more important than pass speed.

Field size:
24 x 24 m

Cone margins:
The distance between the cones within the triangle is 6 m. The three inner cones of the triangles are 12 m apart.

Materials:
9 cones

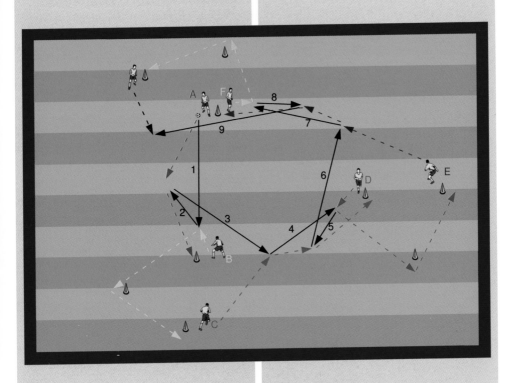

Training Target
- Ball skill (Touch on the ball)

Training Emphasis
- Passing

Training Aspects

Skills involved:	One touch passes, Passing over multiple stations, Passing in a triangle, Short passing, Overlapping, Controlling the ball, Dribbling
Age level:	Under 13 - Adult
Level of play:	Any
Type of training:	Group training
Training structure:	Progression, Main point/Emphasis
Purpose:	Attack behavior, Groups, Improve individual skills
Total number of players:	6 players
Participating players:	Whole team
Training location:	Any
Spatial awareness:	Limited playing field
Duration:	10-15 min
Physiology:	Soccer-specific endurance, Speed endurance, Strength endurance, Power & Speed

Organization:
6 cones are set out as shown. One player starts at each cone. The players in the middle start with a ball.

Process:
Group A, B and C:
Player C passes to B who passes to A and overlaps player A on the way towards the middle cone. Player A then passes to C who lays the ball off with his first touch in space for B to run on to. After that C takes up A's position and B dribbles to the former position of D.

Groups D, E and F have the same passes and runs, i.e. F dribbles after his run to Position C, D to position E and player E runs to position F.

Tip:
Start by running the drill slowly and then speed up. The receiver should always make a small, dynamic dummy run away from the ball before receiving the ball. The drill can be extremely tiring when conducted quickly with only six players.
- Under time pressure, this drill is very game realistic.
- The receiver should call for the ball.
- Pass and run timing is important.
- Players often run faster than their pass.
- Don't forget the runs.
- Demand good strength of pass and pass precision.
- Pass precision is more important than pass speed.
- Concentration must be held at all times.

Field size:
12 x 18 m

Cone margins:
Distance between the outer cones: 12 m
Distance between the middle cones:
6 m from one another and 6 m to the outer
line

Materials:
6 cones

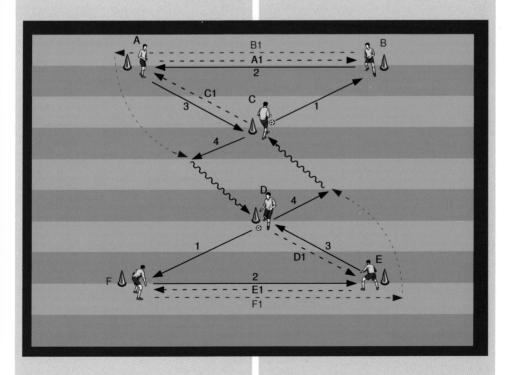

Training Target
- Ball skill (Touch on the ball)

Training Emphasis
- Passing
- Trapping

Training Aspects

Skills involved:	One touch passes, Passing over multiple stations, Passing in a square, Passing in a triangle, Short passing, Overlapping, Controlling the ball, Taking on multiple players, Dribbling
Age level:	13 years - Adult
Level of play:	Advanced
Type of training:	Group training
Training structure:	Warm-up, Progression, Main point/Emphasis
Purpose:	Attack behavior, Groups, Improve individual skills
Total number of players:	7 players
Participating players:	Whole team
Training location:	Any
Spatial awareness:	Limited playing field
Duration:	10-20 min
Physiology:	Soccer-specific endurance, Speed endurance, Power & Speed

Organization:
Set up a box with one cone in the middle. Two of the cones are occupied by two players, the others with only one. There should be a ball at each cone.

Process:
Player A passes to B who moves the ball on to C with his first touch. C then passes for D to run on to, and B runs to C after his pass in order to overlap D.

After that D and B work together as a team and try to out play E with either variation 1 (a trick) or with variation 2 (a pass).
G now passes to E who moves the ball on to C with his first touch. C passes for A to run on to and E overlaps. A and E now try to outplay F with the same two variations as before. E finishes with the ball at G and E takes up the position formerly taken up by F.

Tip:
- This drill is very intensive and tiring and requires a large amount of game intelligence.
- The players will require a certain amount of time to master the drill
- A good touch and passing technique is essential.
- The supporting leg is sometimes too far away from the ball and some players lean back too much.
- Pass and run timing is important
- Demand good strength of pass and pass precision.
- Pass precision is more important than pass speed.
- Concentration must be held at all times.
- The ability to make decisions fast to beat the opposition (with or without team mates)
- Developing creativity together with rehearsing set sequences

- After the drill the players should take up the right positions.

Field size:
18 x 20 m

Cone margins:
Distance vertical: 18 m
Distance horizontal: 20 m

Materials:
5 cones

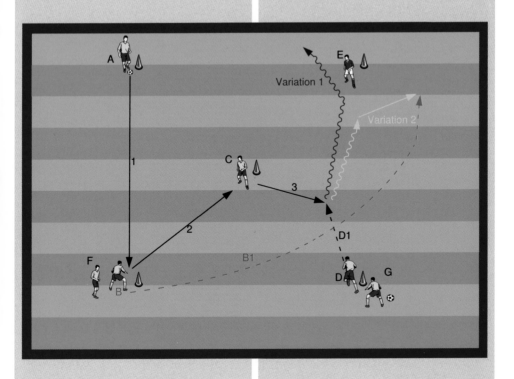

Training Target
• Ball skill (Touch on the ball)

Training Emphasis
• Passing

Training Aspects

Skills involved:	Wall passes, Passing in a rhombus, Short passing, Overlapping, Controlling the ball, Bodyfake, Taking on multiple players,
Age level:	Dribbling
Level of play:	13 years - Adult
Type of training:	Advanced
Training structure:	Group training
Purpose:	Warm-up, Progression, Main point/Emphasis Attack behavior, Groups, Improve
Total number of players:	individual skills
Participating players:	7 players
Training location:	Whole team
Spatial awareness:	Any
Duration:	Limited playing field
Physiology:	10-20 min
	Soccer-specific endurance, Speed endurance, Power & Speed

Organization:
A cross or diamond is formed using 4 cones. One players starts at cones I + II, three players start at cone III and two players start at cone II. There is a ball at cones II + III.

Process:
Player B plays a one-two with player A, controls the ball and the dribbles towards C. Player A overlaps and gives the option of the pass. Player B now has the option of taking on player C or to pass to player A into space for A to run on to. C then moves to give the option of another one-two with D and now they try to take on player F. After the lay off to player D, C overlaps D. The drill is first played to cone I, then cone II and then cones IV and/or III.

Tip:
• This passing drill is very intensive and tiring and requires a large amount of game intelligence.
• Switching the play to the other side, missing out the midfield.
• A good touch and passing technique is essential.
• The supporting leg is sometimes too far away from the ball and some players lean back too much.
• Demand good strength of pass and pass precision.
• Pass precision is more important than pass speed.
• Concentration must be held at all times.
• Anticipation, awareness, reaction, speed of thought and movement with and without the ball are continuously required.

- The aims of this drill are switching from offense to defense, crossing the middle zone quickly and the setting up of new passing situations.

Field size:
20 x 20 m

Cone margins:
Distance from the middle of the diamond:
10 m

Materials:
4 cones

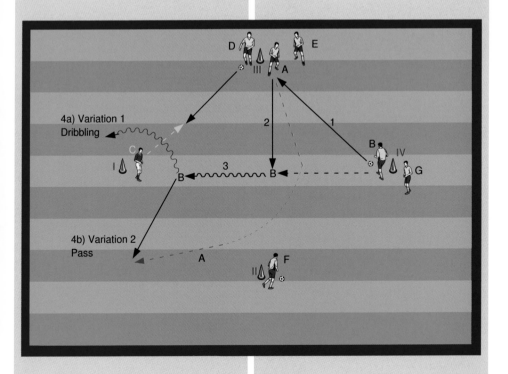

Training Target
- Ball skill (Touch on the ball)

Training Emphasis
- Passing

Training Aspects

Skills involved:	One touch passes, Passing over multiple stations, Passing in a rhombus, Short passing, Overlapping
Age level:	Under 13 - Adult
Level of play:	Advanced
Type of training:	Group training
Training structure:	Warm-up, Progression, Main point/Emphasis
Purpose:	Attack behavior, Groups, Improve individual skills
Total number of players:	6 players
Participating players:	Whole team
Training location:	Any
Spatial awareness:	Limited playing field
Duration:	10-20 min
Physiology:	Soccer-specific endurance, Speed endurance, Power & Speed

Organization:
Set up a diamond/cross as shown. Two or more players start at cones I and IV, one player starts at cones II and III.

Process:
Player A passes to B and overlaps him. Player B passes with his first touch to C. C passes the ball for A to run on to who passes to D and then takes his place behind him. D now starts the same sequence with C and B in the other direction. Players B and C should regularly change places with the other players.

Tip:
Start by running the drill slowly and then speed up. The receiver should always make a small, dynamic dummy run away from or to the side of the ball before receiving the ball. The drill can be extremely tiring when conducted quickly with only six players.
- Under time pressure, this drill is very game realistic.
- The reciever should call for the ball.
- Pass and run timing is important
- Players often run faster than their pass.
- Don't forget the runs.
- Demand good pass precision.

Field size:
20 x 20 m

Cone margins:
10 m from the center to the edge of the
diamond.

Materials:
4 cones

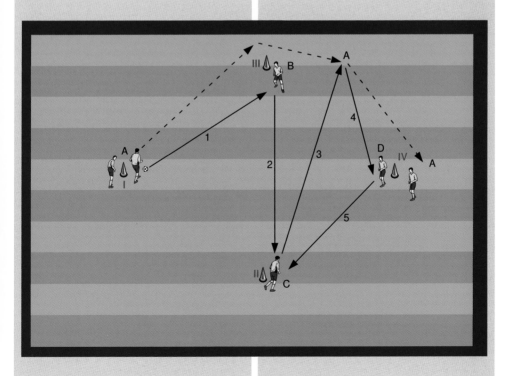

Training Target
- Ball skill (Touch on the ball)

Training Emphasis
- Passing

Training Aspects

Skills involved:	One touch passes, Passing over multiple stations, Passing in a rhombus, Short passing, Overlapping
Age level:	Under 13 - Adult
Level of play:	Advanced, Professional
Type of training:	Group training
Training structure:	Warm-up, Progression, Main point/Emphasis
Purpose:	Attack behavior, Groups, Improve individual skills
Total number of players:	8 players
Participating players:	Whole team
Training location:	Any
Spatial awareness:	Limited playing field
Duration:	10-15 min
Physiology:	Soccer-specific endurance, Speed endurance, Power & Speed

Organization:
Set up a diamond/cross as shown. Two players at each cone. The ball at the start position.

Process:
At least one more player must start behind players A, B, C and D.
A passes to B and then overlaps him. B passes with his first touch for A to run on to. A passes to D and the joins the queue. E starts the same sequence with F and G in the other direction to H.

Players B and C and their partners F & G swap positions with their partners after each sequence.

Tip:
Start by running the drill slowly and then speed up. The receiver should always make a small, dynamic dummy run away from or to the side of the ball before receiving the ball. The drill can be extremely tiring when conducted quickly with only eight players.
- Under time pressure, this drill is very game realistic.
- The reciever should call for the ball.
- Pass and run timing is important
- The passes should take playce simultaneously.
- Players often run faster than their pass.
- Good pass precision ensuresthe balls don't collide.

Field size:
20 x 20 m

Cone margins:
10 m from the center to the edge of the diamond.

Materials:
4 cones

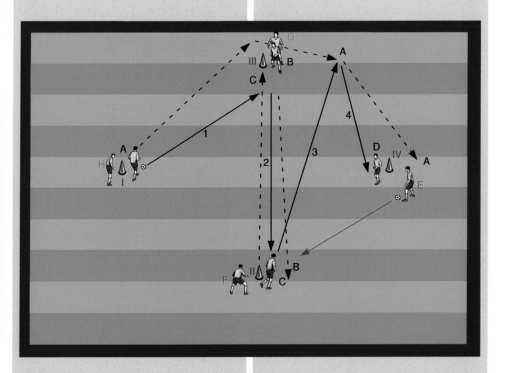

Training Target
- Ball skill (Touch on the ball)

Training Emphasis
- Passing

Training Aspects

Skills involved:	One touch passes, Wall passes, Passing over multiple stations
Age level:	Under 15 - Adult
Level of play:	Advanced, Professional
Type of training:	Group Training
Training structure:	Warm-up, Progression, Main point/Emphasis
Purpose:	Groups, Improve individual skills
Total number of players:	4 players
Participating players:	Whole team
Training location:	Any
Spatial awareness:	Limited playing field
Duration:	10-20 min
Physiology:	Soccer-specific endurance, Speed endurance, Strength endurance, Power & Speed

Organization:
4 cones are set out as shown. The ball starts at the starting cone. One player starts at each cone.

Process:
A starts by playing a long ball on the ground to D. As soon as A has passed, he makes a curved run to B's cone who at the same time makes a short, straight sprint to A and takes over his position. Player D now passes the ball from A back to A to run on to and then moves towards point X, where he receives the ball back from A and passes with his first touch to B. D and C swap positions. Player B starts the same sequence again.

Tip:
Start by running the drill slowly and then speed up. The receiver should always make a small, dynamic dummy run away from or to the side of the ball before receiving the ball. The drill can be extremely tiring when conducted quickly with only four players.
- Under time pressure, this drill is very game realistic.
- The reciever should call for the ball.
- Pass and run timing is important
- Players often run faster than their pass.
- Don't forget the runs.
- Demand good pass precision.
- Pass precision is more important than pass speed.
- Concentration must be held at all times.
- The players will need a certain amount of time until they have mastered the drill.
- A good touch and passing skills are required.
- Anticipation, awareness, reaction, speed of thought and movement with and without the ball are continuously required.

Field size:
15 x 12 m

Cone margins:
Distance vertical: 15 m
Distance between the cones on the field:
3 m vertically/6 m horizontally from the
outer cones.

Materials:
4 cones

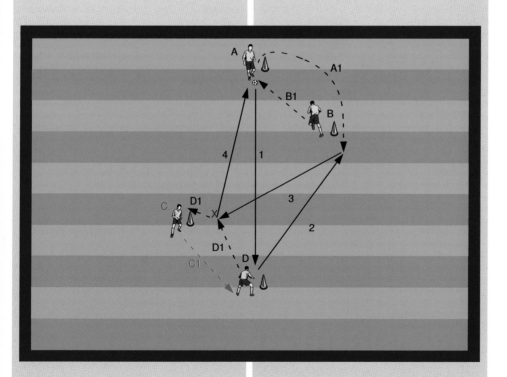

Training Target
• Ball skill (Touch on the ball)

Training Emphasis
• Passing

Training Aspects

Skills involved:	One touch passes, Wall passes, Passing over multiple stations, Passing in a rhombus, Short passing, Long passing, Combinations
Age level:	Under 15 - Adult
Level of play:	Advanced, Professional
Type of training:	Group training
Training structure:	Warm-up, Progression, Main point/Emphasis
Purpose:	Attack behavior, Groups, Improve individual skills
Total number of players:	4 players
Participating players:	Whole team
Training location:	Any
Spatial awareness:	Limited playing field
Duration:	10-20 min
Physiology:	Soccer-specific endurance, Speed endurance, Strength endurance, Power & Speed

Organization:
6 cones are set up as shown. One player per cone. The ball starts at the starting cone.

Process:
A passes a long ball to D and sprints to the outer cone immediately afterwards and plays a one-two with D. D moves to the right-hand outer cone after his pass in order to pass with his first touch to B who has taken up A's position.
A takes up the position from C after two runs at cone I, C goes to cone III, B to A's former position at cone IV and D moves to cone III after his two runs.

In principle:
Long ball - one-two - vertical pass

Tip:
Start by running the drill slowly and then speed up. The receiver should always make a small, dynamic dummy run away from or to the side of the ball before receiving the ball. The drill can be extremely tiring when conducted quickly with only four players.
• Under time pressure, this drill is very game realistic.
• The receiver should call for the ball.
• Pass and run timing is important
• Players often run faster than their pass.
• Don't forget the runs.
• Demand good pass precision.
• Pass precision is more important than pass speed.
• Concentration must be held at all times.
• The players will need a certain amount of time until they have mastered the drill.
• A good touch and passing skills are required.

- Anticipation, awareness, reaction, speed of thought and movement with and without the ball are continuously required.

Field size:
15 x 12 m

Cone margins:
Distance vertical: 15 m
Distance horizontal: 12 m
The two cones in the diamond – 3 m

Materials:
5 cones

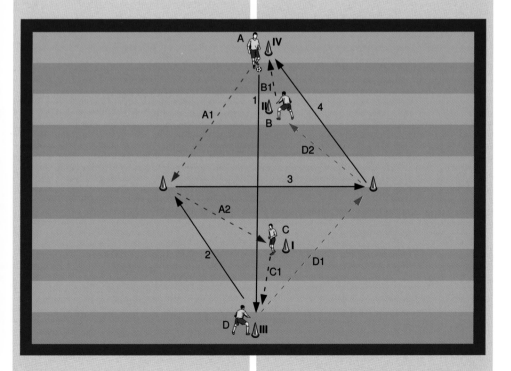

Training Target
- Ball skill (Touch on the ball)

Training Emphasis
- Passing

Training Aspects

Skills involved:	One touch passes, Wall passes, Short passing, Long passing, Controlling the ball, Quick anticipation
Age level:	Under 15 - Adult
Level of play:	Advanced
Type of training:	Group training
Training structure:	Warm-up, Progression, Main point/Emphasis
Purpose:	Attack behavior, Groups, Improve individual skills
Total number of players:	6 players
Participating players:	Whole team
Training location:	Any
Spatial awareness:	Limited playing field
Duration:	10-20 min
Physiology:	Soccer-specific endurance, Speed endurance, Strength endurance, Power & Speed

Organization:
4 cones are laid out as shown. One player starts at each cone. Two further players take up their positions within the field so that they make up a triangle with the other players at the cones (see graphic). D and A have one ball each.

Process:
The drill starts simultaneously on both sides. A and B and D and F play one-twos. A overlaps the defender B and receives a pass from C and passes on to E who is now at the opposite cone (where he has to be standing after the pass and move from group D, E, F). Player A takes up B's former position and B that of A. The same sequence runs in the shape of a triangle in the D, E, F group. D and E swap positions in this group. Player C and F should regularly change positions.

Tip:
Start by running the drill slowly and then speed up. The receiver should always make a small, dynamic dummy run away from or to the side of the ball before receiving the ball. The drill can be extremely tiring when conducted quickly.
- Under time pressure (and when done with 2 balls), this drill is very game realistic.
- The receiver should call for the ball.
- Pass and run timing is important.
- Players often run faster than their pass.
- Don't forget the runs.
- Demand good pass precision.
- Pass precision is more important than pass speed.
- Concentration must be held at all times.
- The players will need a certain amount of time until they have mastered the drill.
- A good touch and passing skills are required.

- Anticipation, awareness, reaction, speed of thought and movement with and without the ball are continuously required.

Field size:
25 x 12 m

Cone margins:
Distance vertical: 25 m
Distance horizontal: 12 m

Materials:
4 cones

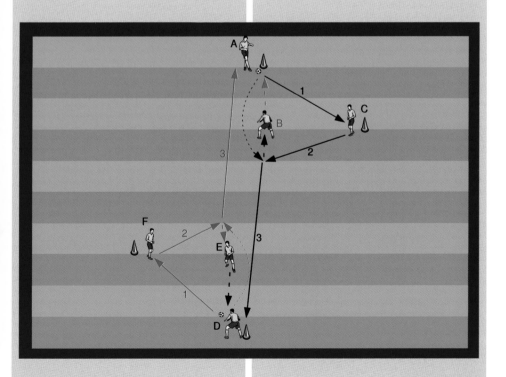

Training Target
- Ball skill (Touch on the ball)

Training Emphasis
- Passing
- Trapping
- Feinting /Trick dribbling

Training Aspects

Skills involved:	One touch passes, Wall passes, Passing over multiple stations, Short passing, Long passing, Controlling the ball, Quick processing, Quick decision making, Dribbling
Age level:	15 years - Adult
Level of play:	Advanced, Professional
Type of training:	Group training
Training structure:	Progression, Main point/Emphasis
Purpose:	Attack behavior, Groups, Improve individual skills
Total number of players:	4 players
Participating players:	Whole team
Training location:	Any
Spatial awareness:	Limited playing field
Duration:	10-20 min
Physiology:	Soccer-specific endurance, Speed endurance, Strength endurance, Power & Speed

Organization:
4 cones are set out as shown. One player starts at each cone. The ball starts at the first cone.

Process:
A starts the sequence by playing a one-two with player B and the playing a long ball on the ground to player C. C turns on the ball and tries to dribble past A with a trick. C and A then swap positions. The same sequence then runs in the other direction, starting with a one-two between players D and A.

Tip:
Start by running the drill slowly and then speed up. The receiver should always make a small, dynamic dummy run away from or to the side of the ball before receiving the ball. The drill can be extremely tiring when conducted quickly with only four players.

- Under time pressure, this drill is very game realistic.
- The reciever should call for the ball.
- Pass and run timing is important
- Players often run faster than their pass.
- Don't forget the runs.
- Demand good pass precision.
- Pass precision is more important than pass speed.
- Concentration must be held at all times.
- The players will need a certain amount of time until they have mastered the drill.
- A good touch and passing skills are required.
- Anticipation, awareness, reaction, speed of thought and movement with and without the ball are continuously required.

Field size:
30 x 10 m

Cone margins:
Distance vertical: 30 m
Distance between the cones A and B / D and C: 6 m

Materials:
4 cones

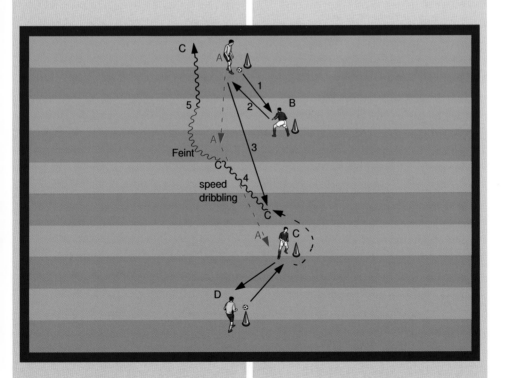

Training Target
- Ball skill (Touch on the ball)

Training Emphasis
- Passing, Trapping
- Dribbling
- Feinting/Trick dribbling

Training Aspects

Skills involved:	One touch passes, Wall passes, Passing over multiple stations, Short passing, Long passing, Bodyfake, Quick processing, One on one
Age level:	Under 15 - Adult
Level of play:	Any
Type of training:	Group training
Training structure:	Warm-up, Progression, Main point/Emphasis
Purpose:	Defense behavior, Attack behavior, Groups, Improve individual skills
Total number of players:	3 players
Participating players:	Whole team
Training location:	Any
Spatial awareness:	Limited playing field
Duration:	10-20 min
Physiology:	Soccer-specific endurance

Organization:
Three cones are set out one behind another as shown. One player starts at each cone. Player C starts with the ball.

Process:
Player C plays a one-two with player B and then hits a ball in the air over player B to A. After controlling the ball, A dribbles at speed towards B who approaches him, and tries to dribbles past him with a trick. A continues to dribble and must then try to go past C as well. A takes up the position at cone I. C goes to cone II and B moves to cone III.

Field size:
30 x 10 m

Cone margins:
15 m

Materials:
3 cones

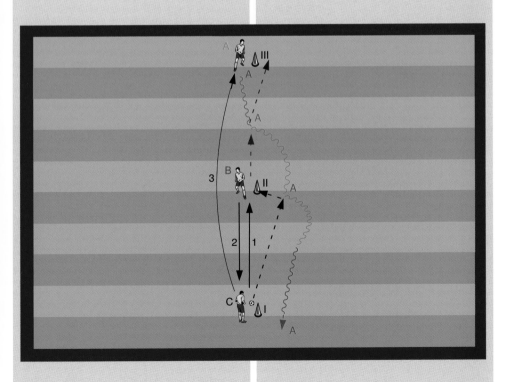

Training Target
- **Ball skill (Touch on the ball)**

Training Emphasis
- **Passing**
- **Trapping**

Training Aspects

Skills involved:	One touch passes, Wall passes, Passing over multiple stations, Passing in a square, Dribbling
Age level:	Under 14 - Adult
Level of play:	Advanced
Type of training:	Group training
Training structure:	Warm-up, Progression, Main point/Emphasis
Purpose:	Groups, Improve individual skills
Total number of players:	4 or more players
Participating players:	Whole team
Training location:	Any
Spatial awareness:	Limited playing field
Duration:	10-20 min
Physiology:	Soccer-specific endurance, Speed endurance, Strength endurance, Power & Speed

Organization:
4 cones are set out as shown. Two or more players start at the first cone. One player starts at cones II + III.

Process:
Player A starts the sequence to player B and the runs diagonally infield while B sprints towards cone III and player D takes up cone II. Player A controls the ball from B with one touch and runs one or two meters with the ball before passing to C. A receives the ball from C again after his diagonal run. After passing the ball C sprints to cone I around cone III. A changes direction after controlling the ball and dribbles at speed back to the start cone.

Tip:
Start by running the drill slowly and then speed up. The receiver should always make a small, dynamic dummy run away from or to the side of the ball before receiving the ball. The drill can be extremely tiring when conducted quickly.
- Under time pressure, this drill is very game realistic.
- The receiver should call for the ball.
- Pass and run timing is important.
- Players often run faster than their pass.
- Don't forget the runs.
- Demand good pass precision.
- Pass precision is more important than pass speed.
- Concentration must be held at all times.
- The players will need a certain amount of time until they have mastered the drill.
- A good touch and passing skills are required.
- Anticipation, awareness, reaction, speed of thought and movement with and without the ball are continuously required.
- Demand top speed at all times.

Field size:
20 x 20 m

Cone margins:
Distance vertical/horizontal 20 m

Materials:
4 cones

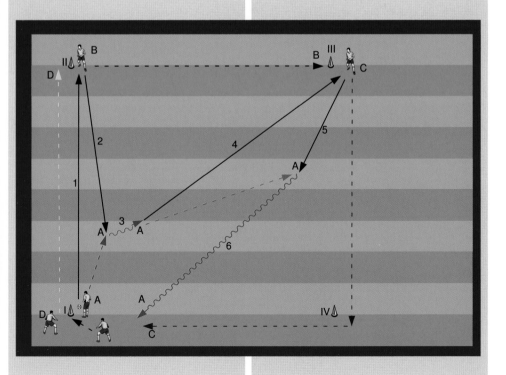

Training Target
- Ball skill (Touch on the ball)

Training Emphasis
- Passing, Trapping,
- Feinting, Trick dribbling
- One on One training

Training Aspects

Skills involved:	One touch passes, Wall passes, Passing over multiple stations, Passing in a square, Dribbling
Age level:	Under 14 - Adult
Level of play:	Advanced
Type of training:	Group training
Training structure:	Warm-up, Progression, Main point/Emphasis
Purpose:	Defense behavior, Attack behavior, Groups, Improve individual skills
Total number of players:	4 or more players
Participating players:	Whole team
Training location:	Any
Spatial awareness:	Limited playing field
Duration:	10-20 min
Physiology:	Soccer-specific endurance, Speed endurance, Power & Speed

Organization:
4 cones are set up as shown. Two or more players start at the start cone, cones I + II have one player each. The ball starts at the start cone.

Process:
Player A starts the passing sequence with a pass to player B. He then runs diagonally infield while B sprints towards cone III and D to cone II. Player A controls the ball played back from B with one touch, runs with the ball for one or two meters and then passes to C. A runs diagonally and receieves the ball from C with C's first touch. C then runs around cone III to cone I where he joins the next sequence. At the same time player E sprints towards player A. A changes direction after controlling the ball and dribbles at speed towards player E and tries to go past him with a trick. The coach decides whether player E should be active or passive. E is replaced by another player and joins at the start position.

Tip:
Start by running the drill slowly and then speed up. The receiver should always make a small, dynamic dummy run away from or to the side of the ball before receiving the ball. The drill can be extremely tiring when conducted quickly with only four players.
- Under time pressure, this drill is very game realistic.
- The receiver should call for the ball.
- Pass and run timing is important.
- Players often run faster than their pass.
- Don't forget the runs.
- Demand good pass precision.
- Pass precision is more important than pass speed.
- Concentration must be held at all times.
- The players will need a certain amount of time until they have mastered the drill.
- A good touch and passing skills are required.

- Anticipation, awareness, reaction, speed of thought and movement with and without the ball are continuously required.
- The drill should be completed at top speed.
- A trick should be used together with successful offensive tackling.

Field size:
20 x 20 m

Cone margins:
Stance vertical/horizontal: 20 m

Materials:
4 cones

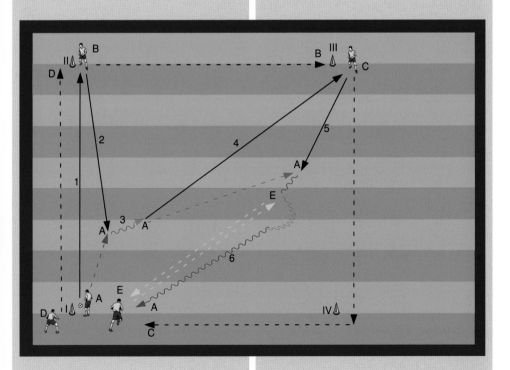

Training Target
- Ball skill (Touch on the ball)

Training Emphasis
- Passing
- Trapping

Training Aspects

Skills involved:	One touch passes, Passing over multiple stations, Passing in a triangle, Short passing, Long passing, Quick processing, Dribbling
Age level:	Under 15 - Adult
Level of play:	Professional
Type of training:	Group training
Training structure:	Warm-up, Progression, Main point/Emphasis
Purpose:	Attack behavior, Groups, Improve individual skills
Total number of players:	5 players
Participating players:	Whole team
Training location:	Any
Spatial awareness:	Limited playing field
Duration:	10-20 min
Physiology:	Soccer-specific endurance, Speed endurance, Power & Speed

Organization:
As shown, set up the drill with 6 cones. A player starts at every cone except cone I. The ball starts at cone III.

Process:
Player E starts the drill from cone II by making a short dummy run away from and then towards the ball. Player D passes him the ball for him to run onto which he passes with his first touch to player A. Player A passes the ball to the player waiting at cone IV and sprints towards cone III passing cone IV on the left side. Arriving at the same cone B passes the ball for A to run onto who passes on to cone I. Player D is now waiting at this cone, having run there after his opening pass to E. From cone I player D passes with his first touch back to A. A controls the ball and takes up the position from D at cone III.

Tip:
Start by running the drill slowly and then speed up. The receiver should always make a small, dynamic dummy run away from or to the side of the ball before receiving the ball. The drill can be extremely tiring when conducted quickly with only four players.
- Under time pressure, this drill is very game realistic.
- The receiver should call for the ball.
- Pass and run timing is important.
- Players often run faster than their pass.
- Don't forget the runs.
- Demand good pass precision.
- Pass precision is more important than pass speed.
- Concentration must be held at all times.
- The players will need a certain amount of time until they have mastered the drill.
- A good touch and passing skills are required.

- Anticipation, awareness, reaction, speed of thought and movement with and without the ball are continuously required.
- This passing and dribbling drill requires a large amount of game intelligence.

Field size:
24 x 12 m

Cone margins:
Distance within the triangles (cones I, II and III): 6 m
Distance vertical:(ones II and VI): 24 m
Distance cones III to IV: 12 m

Materials:
6 cones

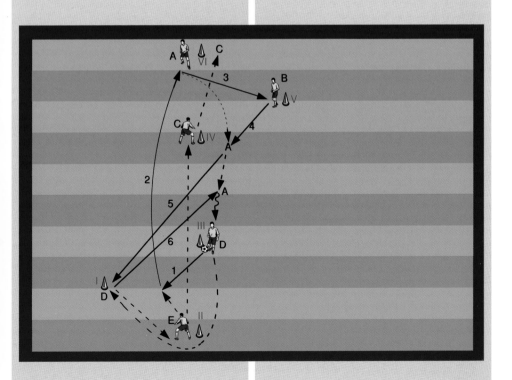

Training Target
- Ball skill (Touch on the ball)

Training Emphasis
- Passing

Training Aspects

Skills involved:	One touch passes, Wall passes, Passing over multiple stations, Short passing, Long passing, Soccer-specific sprint training
Age level:	13 years - Adult
Level of play:	Any
Type of training:	Group training
Training structure:	Warm-up, Progression, Main point/Emphasis
Purpose:	Groups, Improve individual skills
Total number of players:	4 players
Participating players:	Whole team
Training location:	any
Spatial awareness:	Limited playing field
Duration:	10-20 min
Physiology:	Soccer-specific endurance, Power & Speed

Organization:
4 cones are set up as shown. One player at each cone, the ball starts at the start cone.

Process:
Player A hits a long ball in the air to player B. B passes to C with his first touch. C then passes back to B who hits a long ball in the air back to A. After each long ball the two players who played the one-two swap positions at a sprint.

Tip:
Start by running the drill slowly and then speed up. The receiver should always make a small, dynamic dummy run away from or to the side of the ball before receiving the ball.
- Demand good pass precision but also focus on clean lay off before the long balls so that these balls can be played one-touch.
- The reciever must learn to judge the flight of the ball correctly and to adjust his positioning accordingly.
- Pass precision is more important than pass speed.
- Concentration must be held at all times.
- The long ball should be cushioned with the instep.
- The long ball can be player with the instep or the ball of the foot (crossing technique).

Field size:
30 x 15 m

Cone margins:
Distance vertical: 30 m
Distance between the cones by player A to
D / B to C: 7.5m

Materials:
4 cones

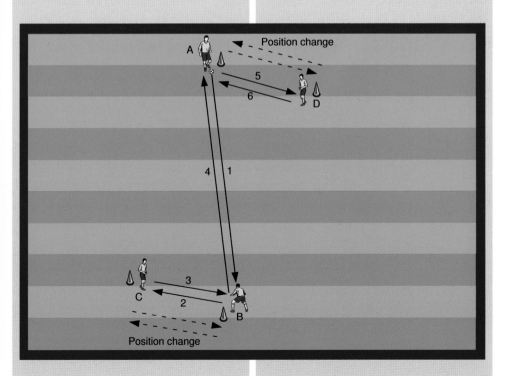

Training Target
- Ball skill (Touch on the ball)

Training Emphasis
- Passing

Training Aspects

Skills involved:	One touch passes, Wall passes, Passing over multiple stations, Short passing, Long passing
Age level:	15 years - Adult
Level of play:	Professional
Type of training:	Group Training
Training structure:	Warm-up, Progression, Main point/Emphasis
Purpose:	Groups, Improve individual skills
Total number of players:	8 players
Participating players:	Whole team
Training location:	Any
Spatial awareness:	Limited playing field
Duration:	10-20 min
Physiology:	Soccer-specific endurance, Power & Speed

Organization:
8 cones are set out as shown. The ball is at the start cone. One player per cone. 4 groups, each with a ball.

Process:
All 4 groups start at the same time and make the same runs.

Example Group I:
A plays a one-two with B and then plays a long ball in the air to player A in group II. At the same time group II does the same and player A from this group hits the long ball to his counterpart in group I.
Groups III + IV complete the same series of passes in their groups. After each long ball the two players within the group swap positions at a sprint.

Tip:
Start by running the drill slowly and then speed up. The receiver should always make a small, dynamic dummy run away from or to the side of the ball before receiving the ball.
- Demand good pass precision but also focus on clean lay off before the long balls so that these balls can be played one-touch.
- Pass precision is more important than pass speed.
- Concentration must be held at all times.
- This drill requires high technical ability under time pressure
- The players should permamnently communicate with one another.
- Make sure that the balls don't hit each other and that the runs are simultaneous.

Field size:
30 x 30 m

Cone margins:
Distance vertical/horizontal: 30 m
Distance cone player A to B: 7.5 m

Materials:
8 cones

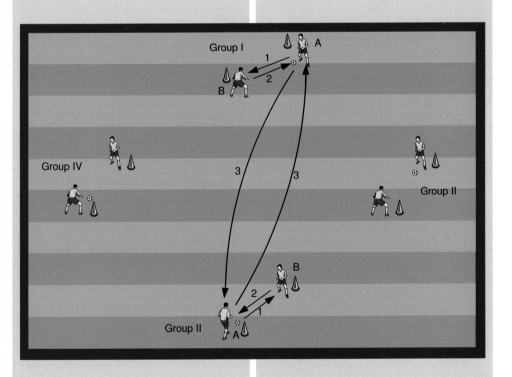

Training Target
- Ball skill (Touch on the ball)

Training Emphasis
- Passing

Training Aspects

Skills involved:	One touch passes, Wall passes, Passing over multiple stations, Short passing, Quick anticipation
Age level:	Under 13 - Adult
Level of play:	Advanced
Type of training:	Group training
Training structure:	Warm-up, Progression, Main point/Emphasis
Purpose:	Attack behavior, Groups, Improve individual skills
Total number of players:	4 players
Participating players:	Whole team
Training location:	Any
Spatial awareness:	Limited playing field
Duration:	10-20 min
Physiology:	Soccer-specific endurance, Speed endurance, Strength endurance, Power & Speed

Organization:
3 cones are set up as shown. Two players start at the first cone. One player at each of the other cones.

Process:
A passes to C. Player B makes a short dummy run towards A (B1) and then sprints to receive the cross-field pass from C. B lays the ball back to C with his first touch and then joins the cone behind A.
A moves to cone III after his pass and takes on the former position from B.
The pass sequence now starts again with C in the other direction.

Tip:
Start by running the drill slowly and then speed up. The receiver should always make a small, dynamic dummy run away from or to the side of the ball before receiving the ball.
- Demand good pass strength and precision.
- Pass precision is more important than pass speed.
- Concentration must be held at all times.
- The timing of the passes and runs is essential.

Field size:
20 x 10 m

Cone margins:
10 m

Materials:
3 cones

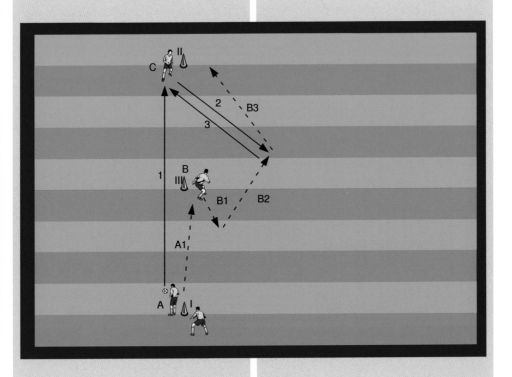

Training Target
- **Ball skill (Touch on the ball)**

Training Emphasis
- **Passing**

Training Aspects

Skills involved:	One touch passes, Wall passes, Passing over multiple stations, Short passing, Long passing, Control, Controlling the ball
Age level:	13 years - Adult
Level of play:	Advanced
Type of training:	Group training
Training structure:	Warm-up, Progression, Main point/Emphasis
Purpose:	Attack behavior, Groups, Improve individual skills
Total number of players:	5 players
Participating players:	Whole team
Training location:	Any
Spatial awareness:	Limited playing field
Duration:	10-20 min
Physiology:	Soccer-specific endurance, Speed endurance, Strength endurance, Power & Speed

Organization:
Set up a passing drill with 4 cones as shown. The first cone whould be occupied by more than one player, One player at each of the other cones.

Process:
Level 1:
Player A begins the drill with a pass on the ground to player B. Player B passes the ball with his first touch to player C who lays the ball off to D, also with his first touch. Each pass should be followed (A to cone II, B to cone III, C to cone IV).

Level 2:
Effectively the same sequence as in level 1, however the sequence is started with a one-two between player A and C, only then is the ball played to player B.

Level 3:
Effectively the same sequence as in level 1, only the first pass is a long ball in the air from A to C.

Alternative:
- The players can take two touches at first
- The passing sequence should flow in both directions

Tip:
- The receiver should always make a small, dynamic dummy run away from or to the side of the ball before receiving the ball.
- Hard, precise passes on the ground.
- When laying the ball off, lightly raise the foot.
- The long ball should be played in such a way that the receiver can immediately lay it off.

Field size:
24 x 6 m

Cone margins:
Distance vertical/cones I to IV: 24 m
Distance horizontal/cones II to III: 10 m
Distance from cones I to II/cones III to IV:
15 m

Materials:
4 cones

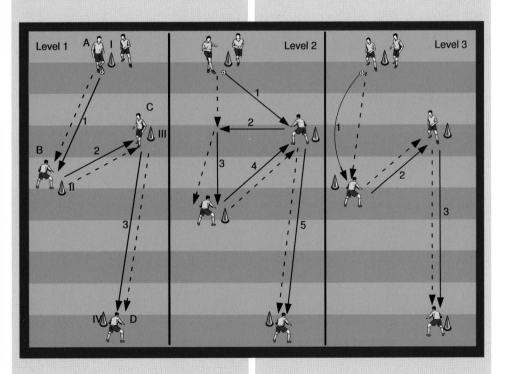

Training Target
- **Ball skill (Touch on the ball)**

Training Emphasis
- **Passing**
- **Trapping**

Training Aspects

Skills involved:	One touch passes, Passing over multiple stations, Short passing, Long passing
Age level:	Under 15- Adult
Level of play:	Advanced
Type of training:	Group Training
Training structure:	Warm-up, Progression, Main point/Emphasis
Purpose:	Attack behavior, Groups,Individual quality
Total number of players:	6 players
Participating players:	Whole team
Training location:	Any
Spatial awareness:	Limited playing field
Duration:	10-20 min
Physiology:	Soccer-specific endurance, Speed endurance, Power & Speed

Organization:
Set up the hexagon as shown. One player per cone, apart from the first cone which is occupied by more than one player. The ball starts here.

Process:
Player A starts the drill with a diagonal pass to player C. He lays the ball off to player B who then plays a cross-field pass to D. Player D also hits a cross-field ball to player F who lays the ball off to player E. The drill ends with a diagonal pass from E to G. The sequence then starts anew in the same fashion. The players all move on one cone clockwise after their passes to take up their new positions. The cross-field ball can be hit on the ground or in the air.

Alternative:
Change direction after 4 sets.

Tip:
- The receiver should always make a small, dynamic dummy run away from or to the side of the ball before receiving the ball.
- Hard, precise passes on the ground.
- When laying the ball off, lightly raise the foot.
- If the corss-field pass is played in the air, then the receiver must be able to lay the ball off with his first touch. I.e. The ball is hit precisely, not too hard no higher than the receiver's chest.
- Communication.
- Correct pass timing and tming of the dummy run away from the pass.

Field size:
30 x 20 m

Cone margins:
Distance between cones at players D and A:
30 m
Distance between cones at players C and E:
20 m

Materials:
6 cones

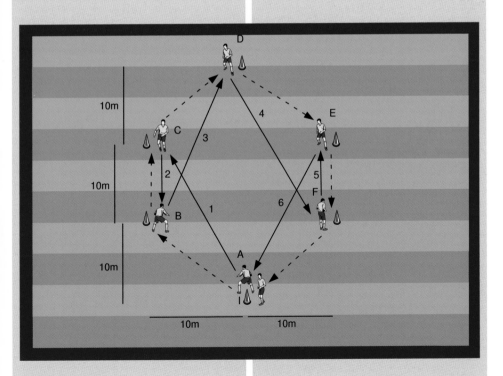

Training Target
- Ball skill (Touch on the ball)

Training Emphasis
- Passing

Training Aspects

Skills involved:	One touch passes, Passing over multiple stations, Short passing, Long passing, Dribbling
Age level:	Under 15 - Adult
Level of play:	Advanced
Type of training:	Group training
Training structure:	Warm-up, Progression, Main point/Emphasis
Purpose:	Attack behavior, Groups, Improve individual skills
Total number of players:	10 players
Participating players:	Whole team
Training location:	Any
Spatial awareness:	Limited playing field
Duration:	10-20 min
Physiology:	Soccer-specific endurance, Speed endurance, Strength endurance, Power & Speed

Organization:
Set up the cones as shown to make two trapezoids. More than one player starts at the first cone. One player at each of other cones. The ball is at the starting cone.

Process:
Player A starts with a cross-field pass to player C, who lays the ball off to player B. Player B then hits a cross-field pass to D who dribbles back to the starting cone at speed. The players all move on one cone clockwise. At the same time, the other group does the same drill starting with a cross-field pass from E to G. The pass can be played on the ground or in the air.

Tip:
- The receiver should always make a small, dynamic dummy run away from or to the side of the ball before receiving the ball.
- Hard, precise passes on the ground.
- When laying the ball off, lightly raise the foot.
- If the cross-field pass is played in the air, then the receiver must be able to lay the ball off with his first touch. I.e. The ball is hit precisely, not too hard no higher than the receiver's chest.
- Make sure that the passes take playce as simultaneously as possible in both groups.
- Communication.

Field size:
36 x 24 m

Cone margins:
Distance between cones at players D to E:
4 m
Distance between cones at players C to
F/B to G: 24 m
Distance between cones I and II: 36 m
Distance between cones III and IV: 12 m

Materials:
8 cones

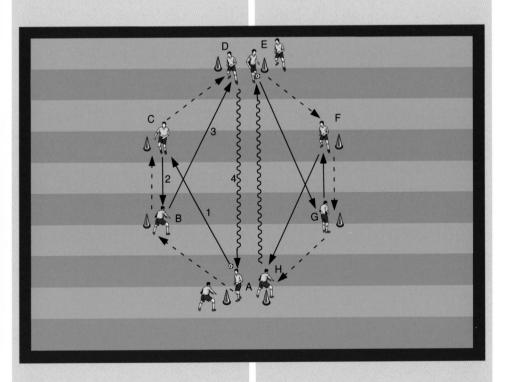

Training Target
- Ball skill (Touch on the ball)

Training Emphasis
- Passing

Training Aspects

Skills involved:	One touch passes, Passing over multiple stations, Short passing, Long passing, Dribbling
Age level:	Under 15 - Adult
Level of play:	Advanced
Type of training:	Group training
Training structure:	Warm-up, Progression, Main point/Emphasis
Purpose:	Attack behavior, Groups, Improve individual skills
Total number of players:	10 players
Participating players:	Whole team
Training location:	Any
Spatial awareness:	Limited playing field
Duration:	10-20 min
Physiology:	Soccer-specific endurance, Speed endurance, Strength endurance, Power & Speed

Organization:
Set up the cones as shown to make two trapezoids. More than one player starts at the first cone. One player at each of other cones. The ball is at the starting cone.

Process:
Players A and E start the drill at the same time. Player A hits a cross-field pass to C, who lays the ball off to B. B then hits a cross-field pass to D who controls the ball and dribbles at speed back to the starting position. As the group with players E and F have hit the same passes, the runs from players D and H cross. Just before, the two players call and then pass the ball in order to return to their start positions. After each pass, each player moves on one cone. The cross-field ball can be played on the ground or hit in the air.

Tip:
- The receiver should always make a small, dynamic dummy run away from or to the side of the ball before receiving the ball.
- Hard, precise passes on the ground.
- When laying the ball off, lightly raise the foot.
- If the cross-field pass is played in the air, then the receiver must be able to lay the ball off with his first touch. I.e. The ball is hit precisely, not too hard no higher than the receiver's chest.
- Make sure that the passes take playce as simultaneously as possible in both groups.
- Communication.

Field size:
36 x 24 m

Cone margins:
Distance between cones at players D to E:
4 m
Distance between cones at players C to F/B
to G: 24 m
Distance between cones I and II: 36 m
Distance between cones III and IV: 12 m

Materials:
8 cones

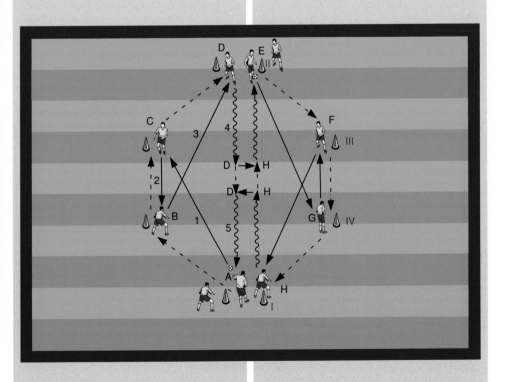

Training Target
- Ball skill (Touch on the ball)

Training Emphasis
- Passing

Training Aspects

Skills involved:	One touch passes, Wall passes, Passing over multiple stations, Short passing, Long passing, Dribbling
Age level:	Under 15 - Adult
Level of play:	Advanced
Type of training:	Group training
Training structure:	Warm-up, Progression, Main point/Emphasis
Purpose:	Attack behavior, Groups, Improve individual skills
Total number of players:	10 players
Participating players:	Whole team
Training location:	Any
Spatial awareness:	Limited playing field
Duration:	10-20 min
Physiology:	Soccer-specific endurance, Speed endurance, Strength endurance, Power & Speed

Organization:
Set up the cones as shown to make two trapezoids. More than one player starts at the first cone. One player at each of other cones. The ball is at the starting cone.

Process:
Players A and E start at the same time so that the groups run simultaneously. A starts the sequence of passes with a cross-field ball to C, who lays the ball off to B. Player B then hits a cross-field pass to D. D plays a one-two with player C, but can be tackled by F. He then dribbles at speed back to the start position. Player F then goes back to his position. Player B plays the role of defender in the other group. After each pass, the players move on one cone in a clockwise direction. The cross-field pass can be played on the ground or in the air.

Tip:
- The receiver should always make a small, dynamic dummy run away from or to the side of the ball before receiving the ball.
- Hard, precise passes on the ground.
- When laying the ball off, lightly raise the foot.
- If the cross-field pass is played in the air, then the receiver must be able to lay the ball off with his first touch. I.e. The ball is hit precisely, not too hard no higher than the receiver's chest.
- Make sure that the passes take playce as simultaneously as possible in both groups so that the players who have left the group for a short time because of the one-two, can take up their positions again, in order to take part in the passing drill.

Field size:
36 x 24 m

Cone margins:
Distance between cones at players D to E:
4 m
Distance between cones at players C to F/B
to G: 24 m
Distance between cones I and II: 36 m
Distance between cones III and IV: 12 m

Materials:
8 cones

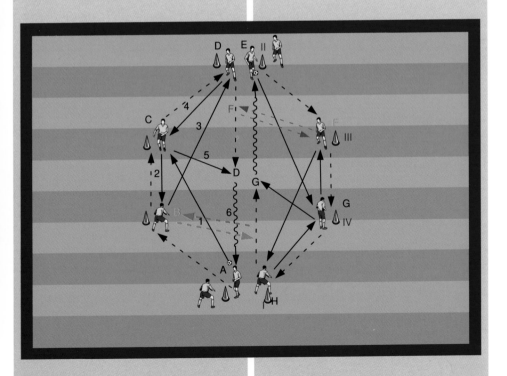

Training Target
- Ball skill (Touch on the ball)

Training Emphasis
- Passing
- Shooting

Training Aspects

Skills involved:	One touch passes, Passing over multiple stations, Short passing
Age level:	13 years - Adult
Level of play:	Advanced
Type of training:	Group training
Training structure:	Warm-up, Progression, Main point/Emphasis
Purpose:	Attack behavior, Goalkeeper behaviors, Groups, Improve individual skills
Total number of players:	6 players
Participating players:	Whole team
Training location:	Any
Spatial awareness:	Limited playing field
Duration:	10-20 min
Physiology:	Soccer-specific endurance, Power & Speed
Goalkeeping:	1 goalie

Organization:
Set up the hexagon with cones as shown. One player per cone, the ball at the start cone.

Process:
The passing drill starts with a cross-field ball from A to C. C lays the ball off to player B who hits a cross-field pass to D. D lays the ball off to E who hits a cross-field pass to C. C sprints away from his cone after his pass to B and can now take a shot at goal. The players' runs form a circle, i.e. each player moves on one cone after his pass/shot.

After each player has had a shot at the goal, the drill is repeated in the other direction, i.e. the first pass is from A to E, who will then take a shot at the goal.

Tip:
- The receiver should always make a small, dynamic dummy run away from or to the side of the ball before receiving the ball.
- Hard, precise passes on the ground.
- When laying the ball off, lightly raise the foot.
- Time the runs.
- Hit the target!

Field size:
40 x 50 m

Cone margins:
- The receiver should always make a small, dynamic dummy run away from or to the side of the ball before receiving the ball.
- Hard, precise passes on the ground.
- When laying the ball off, lightly raise the foot.
- Time the runs.
- Hit the target!

Materials:
1 normal goal, 6 cones

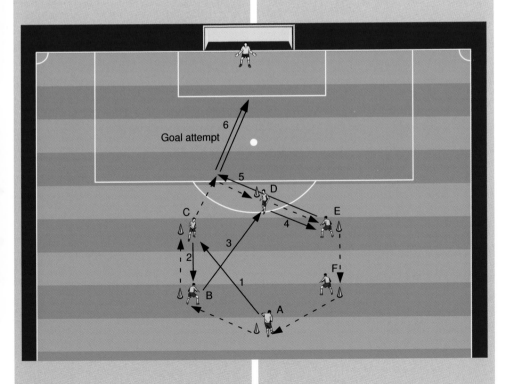

Training Target
- Ball skill (Touch on the ball)

Training Emphasis
- Passing
- Shooting

Training Aspects

Skills involved:	One touch passes, Wall passes, Passing over multiple stations, Passing in a square, Short passing, Inside of the laces passing, Laces, Advanced passing, Volley, Heading while in motion, Wing play without opponents
Age level:	13 years - Adult
Level of play:	Advanced
Type of training:	Group training
Training structure:	Main point/Emphasis
Purpose:	Attack behavior, Free kicks, Goalkeeper behaviors, Groups, Improve individual skills
Total number of players:	7 players
Participating players:	Whole team
Training location:	Any
Spatial awareness:	Limited playing field
Duration:	10-20 min
Physiology:	Soccer-specific endurance, Speed endurance, Power & Speed
Goalkeeping:	1 goalie

Organization:
Set up a cone box as shown. Each cone should be occupied by a player.
Three more players should be positioned as follows: Two players to the side of the 18 yard box, one player to the side of the goal on the goal line.

Process:
The drill starts with a cross-field pass from player A to player C within the box. Player C lays the ball off to player B who passes diagonally to player D. D lays the ball off for player C who, after a short sprint, shoots at the goal.

After the shot at the goal, D sprints into the box and either finishes a:

a) cross from G
b) cross from E
or
c) a backpass from F.
Every player then moves on one position.

Tip:
- The player waiting for the ball should always make a short, quick dummy run away from the ball before receiving it.
- The passes should be played hard along the ground
- The player should lift his foot slightly when laying the ball off
- Timing is important when making runs in the box
- The crosses and backpasses should be hit hard

Field size:
40 x 50 m

Cone margins:
Distance vertical/horizontal: 10 m

Materials:
4 cones

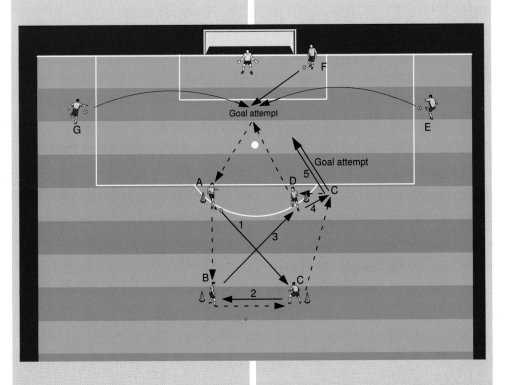

Training Target
- Ball skill (Touch on the ball)

Training Emphasis
- Passing
- Shooting

Training Aspects

Skills involved:	One touch passes, Wall passes, Passing over multiple stations, Short passing, Inside of the laces passing, Laces, Advanced passing, Volley, Heading while in motion, Wing play without opponents
Age level:	13 years - Adult
Level of play:	Advanced
Type of training:	Group training
Training structure:	Main point/Emphasis
Purpose:	Attack behavior, Free kicks, Goalkeeper behaviors, Groups, Improve individual skills
Total number of players:	7 players
Participating players:	Whole team
Training location:	Any
Spatial awareness:	Limited playing field
Duration:	10-20 min
Physiology:	Soccer-specific endurance, Speed endurance, Power & Speed
Goalkeeping:	1 goalie

Organization:
Set up a cone box as shown. Each cone should be occupied by a player. Three more players should be positioned as follows: Two players to the side of the 18 yard box, one player to the side of the goal on the goal line.

Process:
The drill begins with a diagonal pass from A to C within the 10m box. Player C lays the ball off to D who then passes diagonally to player B. B lays the ball off for player C who, after a short sprint, shoots at the goal.

Immediately after the goal attempt, C sprints into the box and crosses positions with C who has positioned himself ready for the next move and then they either finishes a:

a) cross from G
b) cross from E
or
c) a backpass from F.
Every player then moves on one position.

Tip:
- The player waiting for the ball should always make a short, quick dummy run away from the ball before receiving it.
- The passes should be played hard along the ground
- The player should lift his foot slightly when laying the ball off
- Timing is important when making runs in the box
- The crosses and backpasses should be hit hard

Field size:
40 x 50 m

Cone margins:
Distance: 10 m

Materials:
1 normal goal, 4 cones

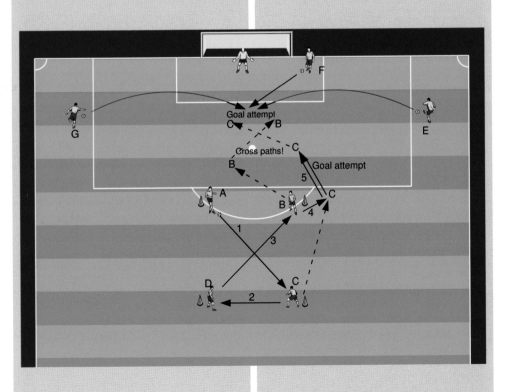

Training Target
- **Ball skill (Touch on the ball)**

Training Emphasis
- **Passing**
- **Shooting**

Training Aspects

Skills involved:	One touch passes, Wall passes, Passing over multiple stations, Short passing, Inside of the laces passing, Laces, Advanced passing, Volley, Heading while in motion, Wing play without opponents
Age level:	13 years - Adult
Level of play:	Advanced
Type of training:	Group training
Training structure:	Main point/Emphasis
Purpose:	Attack behavior, Goalkeeper behaviors, Groups, Improve individual skills
Total number of players:	7 players
Participating players:	Whole team
Training location:	Any
Spatial awareness:	Limited playing field
Duration:	10-20 min
Physiology:	Soccer-specific endurance, Speed endurance, Power & Speed
Goalkeeping:	1 goalie

Organization:
Set up a cone box as shown. Each cone should be occupied by a player. Three further players should be positioned as follows: Two players to the side of the 18 yard box, one player to the side of the goal on the goal line.

Process:
The drill starts with a one-two between player A and player D. A passes the laid-off ball diagonally to C who lays the ball off to D. D passes diagonally to B and at the same time C sprints to the right hand corner of the 18 yard box where he receives a pass from B and takes a shot at the goal.

Immediately after the goal attempt, B sprints into the box and crosses positions with C who has positioned himself ready for the next move and then they either finish with a:
a) cross from G
b) cross from E
or
c) a backpass from F.
Every player then moves on one position.

Tip:
- The player waiting for the ball should always make a short, quick dummy run away from the ball before receiving it.
- The passes should be played hard along the ground.
- The player should lift his foot slightly when laying the ball off.
- Timing is important when making runs in the box.

- The crosses and backpasses should be hit hard.

Field size:
40 x 50 m

Cone margins:
Distance: 10 m

Materials:
4 cones

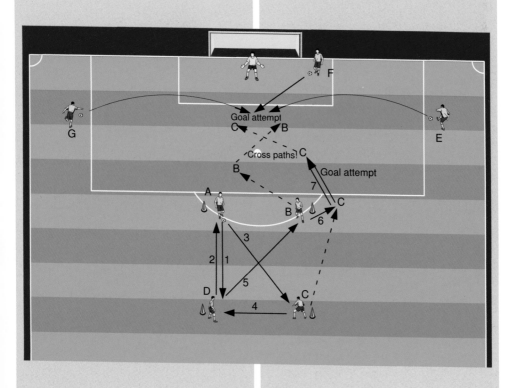

Training Target
- Ball skill (Touch on the ball)

Training Emphasis
- Passing
- Shooting

Training Aspects

Skills involved:	One touch passes, Wall passes, Passing over multiple stations, Passing in a square, Short passing, Inside of the laces passing, Laces, Advanced passing, Volley, Heading while in motion, Wing play without opponents
Age level:	13 years - Adult
Level of play:	Advanced
Type of training:	Group training
Training structure:	Main point/Emphasis
Purpose:	Attack behavior, Goalkeeper behaviors, Groups, Improve individual skills
Total number of players:	7 players
Participating players:	Whole team
Training location:	Any
Spatial awareness:	Limited playing field
Duration:	10-20 min
Physiology:	Soccer-specific endurance, Power & Speed
Goalkeeping:	1 goalie

Organization:
Set up a cone box as shown. Each cone should be occupied by a player. Three further players should be positioned as follows: Two players to the side of the 18 yard box, one player to the side of the goal on the goal line.

Process:
Player A starts by passing a cross-field pass to player C. C lays the ball off to D who in turn hits a cross-field pass to player B. Player B passes to A who sets up player C for a shot at the goal.

As soon as C has taken his shot, player B sprints into the box and crosses with player C who has now taken up a new position and then either finishes with a:

a) cross from G
b) cross from E
or
c) a backpass from F.
Every player then moves on one position.

Tip:
- The player waiting for the ball should always make a short, quick dummy run away from the ball before receiving it.
- The passes should be played hard along the ground.
- The player should lift his foot slightly when laying the ball off.
- Timing is important when making runs in the box.
- The crosses and backpasses should be hit hard.

Field size:
40 x 50 m

Cone margins:
Distance (horizontal and vertical): 10 m

Materials:
1 normal goal, 4 cones

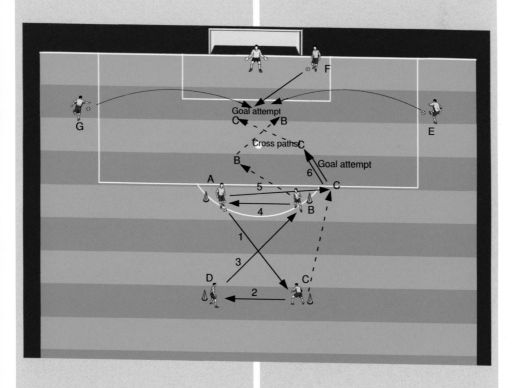

Training Target
- Ball skill (Touch on the ball)

Training Emphasis
- Passing
- Shooting

Training Aspects

Skills involved:	Wall passes, Passing over multiple stations, Short passing, Long passing
Age level:	Under 15 - Adult
Level of play:	Advanced
Type of training:	Group training
Training structure:	Main point/Emphasis
Purpose:	Groups, Improve individual skills
Total number of players:	6 or more players
Participating players:	Whole team
Training location:	Any
Spatial awareness:	Limited playing field
Duration:	15-20 min
Physiology:	Soccer-specific endurance, Speed endurance, Strength endurance, Power & Speed
Goalkeeping:	1 goalie

Organization:
Set up the exercise as shown with 4 cones. Two or more players can stand at the start cone.

Process:
Player A passes a long ball (on the ground or in the air) to player B and then sprints after his pass. Player B lays the ball off for A to run onto who then passes to C. C passes a short pass to B. At the same time, player D sprints towards the 18 yard box. Player B passes the ball into space, down the middle for D to run on to, he should reach the ball approx. 14 - 18m from goal. D shoots at goal, and then takes up the position from player A. All players then move on one position.

Tip:
Start by running the drill slowly and then increase the speed. The player waiting for the ball should always make a short, quick dummy run away from the ball before controlling it. At a high tempo and with just 4 players this exercise can be extremely tiring.
- Under time contrictions, this is a very realistic and challenging passing drill
- The players waiting for the ball should call for each ball
- The timing of the passand the timing of the start are key.
- Precision is more important than speed.
- Concentration must be held at all times.
- The passes should be played hard along the ground
- The player should lift his foot slightly when laying the ball off
- Goals!

Field size:
One half

Cone margins:
Distance between cones I - II: 40 m
Distance between cones II - III: 10 m
Distance between cones III - IV: 10 m

Materials:
1 normal goal, 4 cones

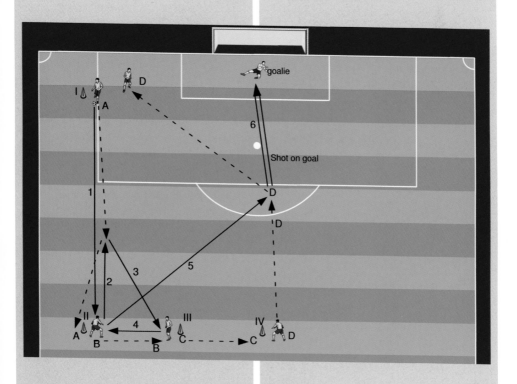

Training Target
- Ball skill (Touch on the ball)

Training Emphasis
- Passing
- Shooting

Training Aspects

Skills involved:	One touch passes, Passing over multiple stations, Passing in different formations, Short passing, Control, Combining technical skill with movement
Age level:	Adult (from 18 years on)
Level of play:	Professional
Type of training:	Team training
Training structure:	Main point/Emphasis
Purpose:	Cooperation within the team
Total number of players:	5 players
Participating players:	Whole team
Training location:	Any
Spatial awareness:	Half-field
Duration:	15-20 min
Physiology:	Soccer-specific endurance
Goalkeeping:	1 goalie

Organization:
The cones are set out as shown. Two or more players can start at the start cone. One players stands at each of the other cones.

Process:
One touch soccer is played in the pentagon followed by a deep pass (1-6) into the hexagon. The player receiving the long pass controls the ball on the turn and starts passes 7-12. Pass (13) is a lateral pass to player A. A controls the ball and dribbles quickly (14) before passing to B (15). B lays the ball off into the path of A (16) who shoots at the goal (17) from around 14-17 meters.

After the completed phase of play, each player moves on one cone. Player A becomes the player laying the ball off (formerly B) and B joins the drill at the beginning.

Tip:
Start by practicing the exercise slowly and then raise the speed of the passing. The players waiting for the ball should always make a short, powerful dummy run (either sidewards or backwards) before receiving each pass.
- The players will need a certain amount of time until they have memorized the movements.
- Good technique, touch and passing is important.
- The strength and precision of the pass.
- Precision is more imporatant than speed.
- Concentration must be held at all times.
- Communication is continuously important.
- Anticipation, awareness, reaction, speed of movement with and without the ball are regularly tested.
- Practise of rehearsed phases of play.

Field size:
One Half

Cone margins:
Distance between cones in pentagon and
hexagon: 6 m
Position of Player B: Cone on the 18 yard
box line, in line with the front post.
Position of Player A: Cone is central in the
"D"
Distance from pentagon to hexagon: 15 m

Materials:
1 normal goal, 13 cones

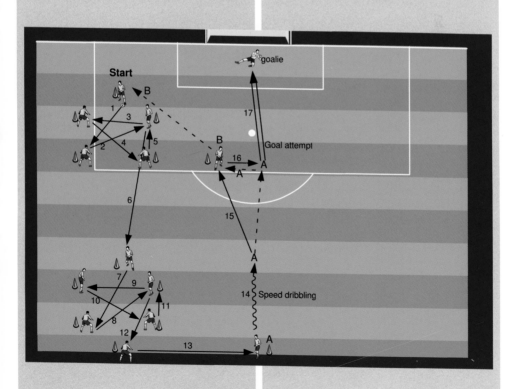

Training Target
- Ball skill (Touch on the ball)

Training Emphasis
- Passing
- Shooting

Training Aspects

Skills involved:	One touch passes, Wall passes, Passing over multiple stations, Short passing, Control, Attacking down the middle
Age level:	Under 15 - Adult
Level of play:	Advanced, Professional
Type of training:	Group training
Training structure:	Main point/Emphasis, End
Purpose:	Attack behavior, Groups, Improve individual skills
Total number of players:	6 or more players
Participating players:	Whole team
Training location:	Any
Spatial awareness:	Half-field
Duration:	10-20 min
Physiology:	Soccer-specific endurance, Power & Speed
Goalkeeping:	1 goalie

Organization:
Five cones are laid out as shown. Several players stand at the starting cones with a ball. One player stands at each other cone plus a goalkeeper.

Process:
Player A passes to B, who lays the ball off for A to run on to and moves towards D. A passes to C, C touches the ball off to B and C runs towards the goal. B passes to D who passes to C in space. C shoots.

All players move on one position apart from D who joins the starting position on the parallel exercise.

Alternative:
- Player A passes straight to C, who passes to B, etc.
- Player A passes to D after the one-two with B and he passes to C.
- Player A passes the first ball deep to D. D can choose if he lays the ball off to C or tries to score alone.

Tip:
The focus is on developing variable, fast passing with goal attempts through the middle.
- Good technique, touch and passing is important.
- Strength and precision of the pass is important.
- Precision is more imporatant than speed.
- Concentration must be held at all times.
- Communication is continuously important.

- Anticipation, awareness, reaction, speed of movement with and without the ball are regularly tested.
- Practise of rehearsed phases of play, short passing and variable combination soccer.
- Goal scoring.

Field size:
One Half

Cone margins:
7-8 m

Materials:
1 normal goal, 5 cones

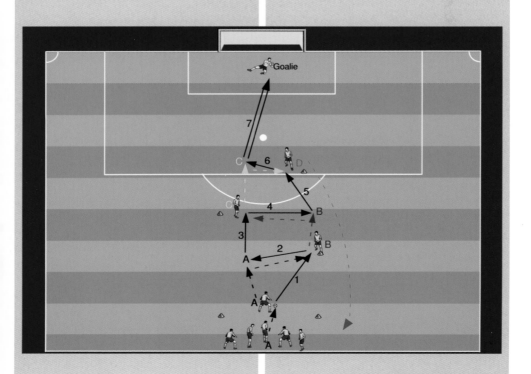

Training Target
- Ball skill (Touch on the ball)

Training Emphasis
- Passing
- Shooting

Training Aspects

Skills involved:	One touch passes, Wall passes, Passing over multiple stations, Short passing, Control, Attacking down the middle, Combinations
Age level:	Under 15 - Adult
Level of play:	Advanced, Professional
Type of training:	Group training
Training structure:	Main point/Emphasis, End
Purpose:	Attack behavior, Groups, Improve individual skills
Total number of players:	12 players, 13 or more players
Participating players:	Whole team
Training location:	Any
Spatial awareness:	Half-field, Limited playing field
Duration:	15-25 min
Physiology:	Soccer-specific endurance, Speed endurance, Strength endurance, Power & Speed
Goalkeeping:	2 goalies

Organization:
Two courses with 4 cones are set up as shown. Several players stand at the cones with a ball. One player stands at each of the other cones. One goalkeeper.

Process:
Player A passes to B, B lays the ball off in space to A and runs to D. A passes to C, C touches the ball off to B and B runs towards the goal. B passes to D who passes for C to run on to. C shoots. All players move on one position apart from D who joins the starting position on the parallel exercise. The phase of plays take place on both courses at the same time.

Alternative:
- Player A passes straight to C, who passes to B, etc.
- A passes to D after the one-two with B and he passes to C.
- layer A passes the first ball deep to D. D can choose if he lays the ball off to C or tries to score alone.

Tip:
The focus is on developing variable, fast passing with goal attempts through the middle.
- Good technique, touch and passing is important.
- Strength and precision of the pass is important.
- Precision is more imporatant than speed.
- Concentration must be held at all times.
- Communication is continuously important.

- Anticipation, awareness, reaction, speed of movement with and without the ball are regularly tested.
- Practise of rehearsed phases of play, short passing and variable combination soccer.
- Goal scoring.

Field size:
One Half

Cone margins:
7-8 m

Materials:
2 normal goal, 8 cones

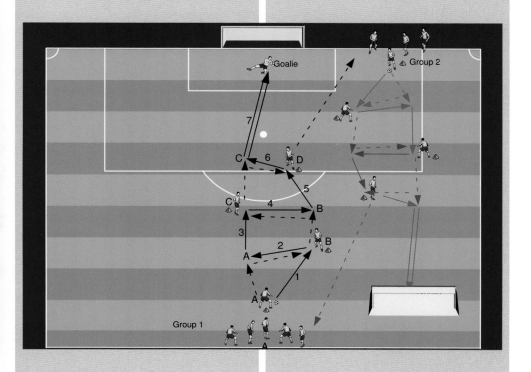

Training Target
- Ball skill (Touch on the ball)

Training Emphasis
- Passing

Training Aspects

Skills involved:	One touch passes, Passing over multiple stations, Short passing
Age level:	17 years - Adult
Level of play:	Advanced
Type of training:	Group training
Training structure:	Warm-up, Progression, Main point/Emphasis
Purpose:	Attack behavior, Groups, Improve individual skills
Total number of players:	6 players
Participating players:	Whole team
Training location:	Any
Spatial awareness:	Limited playing field
Duration:	10-20 min
Physiology:	Soccer-specific endurance, Speed endurance, Strength endurance, Power & Speed

Organization:
Three cones are laid out as shown. Two players stand at the starting cones, two players stand at the middle cones and at the cone nearest to the goal.

Process:
A (1) passes to C at which point B moves 2 to 3 meters to the side to receive the pass from C (2) and then passes to D (3) with his first touch. The same combination of passes now flows in the other direction.

D passes (4) to A, who has now moved to the middle cone after his first pass. D runs to A after his pass, also to the middle cone. A lays the ball of in space for C to run onto. C has moved after pass 3 and now passes to player F (6), etc.

C follows the ball to F after his pass (6). A takes up the position from B and D takes over the position from D.

Now the same combination of passes flows again, starting at F.

Tip:
- The exercise requires lots of running and a large amount of inteligence.
- The players will need a certain amount of time until they have managed to memorise the movements.
- Good technique and combination passing is necessary.
- Precision is more important than speed.
- Concentration must be held at all times.
- Communication is continuously important.
- Anticipation, awareness, reaction, speed of movement with and without the ball are regularly tested.
- Practise of rehearsed phases of play.

Field size:
20 x 8 m

Cone margins:
Distance between cones: 10 m

Materials:
3 cones

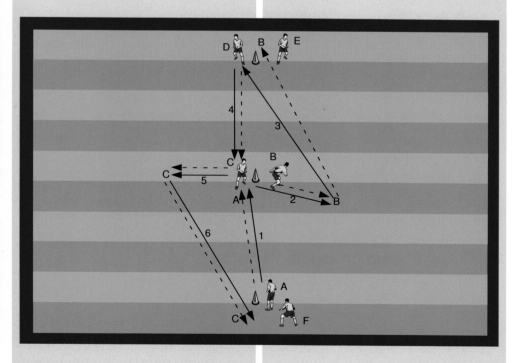

Training Target
- Ball skill (Touch on the ball)

Training Emphasis
- Passing

Training Aspects

Skills involved:	One touch passes, Passing over multiple stations, Short passing
Age level:	17 years - Adult
Level of play:	Advanced, Professional
Type of training:	Group training
Training structure:	Warm-up, Progression, Main point/Emphasis
Purpose:	Attack behavior, Groups, Improve individual skills
Total number of players:	5 players
Participating players:	Whole team
Training location:	Any
Spatial awareness:	Limited playing field
Duration:	10-20 min
Physiology:	Soccer-specific endurance, Speed endurance, Strength endurance, Power & Speed

Organization:
Three cone goals are laid out as shown. Two or more players stand at the starting cones and middle cones. One player stands at the cone nearest to the goal.

Process:
A starts with a pass (1) to B whose first movement is towards A. B lays the ball off to A (2) in space and then moves after passing the ball. A passes to C with one touch (3) who passes with one touch to B in space (4). B passes to D (5).

A runs to the middle cone and B takes up the positon form D. C stays at the middle cone. B joins the start cone with D after his three runs, etc

The same combination of passes then begins again with D. C takes over the three runs from B and A takes over the role from C.

Tip:
- The exercise requires lots of running and a large amount of inteligence.
- The payers will need a certain amount of time until they have managed to memorise the movements.
- The strength and precision of the pass are important.
- Precision is more important than speed.
- Concentration must be held at all times.
- Communication is continuously important.
- Anticipation, awareness, reaction, speed of movement with and without the ball are regularly tested.
- Practise of rehearsed phases of play.

Field size:
20 x 8 m

Cone margins:
Distance between the cones: 10 m

Materials:
3 cones

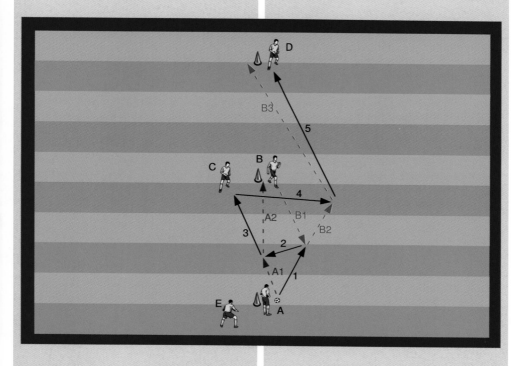

Training Target
- **Ball skill (Touch on the ball)**

Training Emphasis
- **Passing**
- **Shooting**

Training Aspects

Skills involved:	One touch passes, Passing over multiple stations, Short passing, Control, Soccer-specific sprint, coordination and shooting training, Attacking down the middle
Age level:	17 years - Adult
Level of play:	Advanced, Professional
Type of training:	Group training, Team training
Training structure:	Main point/Emphasis, End
Purpose:	Attack behavior, Groups, Improve individual skills
Total number of players:	10 or more players
Participating players:	Whole team
Training location:	Any
Spatial awareness:	Limited playing field
Duration:	10-20 min
Physiology:	Soccer-specific endurance, Explosiveness
Goalkeeping	1 goalie

Organization:
Three cones are laid out as shown. Two or more players stand at the start cones. 2 players stand at the middle cones. One player stands at the cones nearest the goalkeeper. One goalkeeper in goal.

Process:
The left and right groups take turns to complete the practiced pass and move combinations I & II with a resulting shot at goal. The player who starts decides which variation will be played.

Variation I:
A (1) passes to C, B moves two to three meters to the side to be able to pass the ball from C to D with one touch. D attempts to score.
A runs to the middle cone and B takes up the positon from D. C stays at the middle cone. D joins the start cone, etc.

Variation II:
Z passes (1) to X whose first movement is towards player Z. X (2) then lays the ball into space for Z and then moves after passing the ball. Z passes (3) to Y with his first touch, Y then passes with his first touch in space (4) to X. X passes to W (5). Player W tries to score. Z joins the middle cone after his pass. Y stays where he is. X joins the last cone with W after his three runs. W joins the start cone, etc.

Alternative:
- Goal scoring competition. Both teams count their goals scored.
- A second goal can be introduced.

Tip:

The focus is on a variation of fast passing combinations through the middle.

- Good technique, touch and passing is important.
- Strength and precision of the pass is important.
- Precision is more imporatant than speed.
- Communication is continuously important.
- Anticipation, awareness, reaction, speed of movement with and without the ball are regularly tested.
- Practice of rehearsed phases of play, short passing and variable combination soccer.
- Goal scoring.

Field size:
One half

Cone margins:
12 m

Materials:
1 normal goal, 6 cones

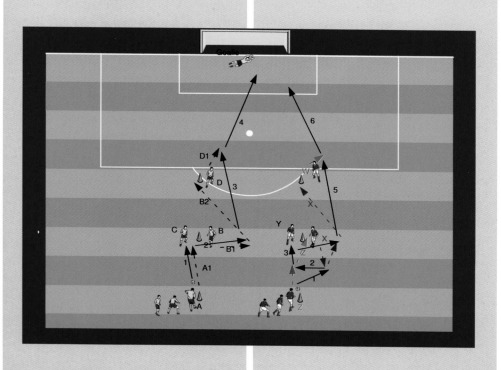

Training Target
- Ball skill (Touch on the ball)

Training Emphasis
- Passing
- Shooting

Training Aspects

Skills involved:	One touch passes, Passing over multiple stations, Short passing, Control, Soccer-specific sprint, coordination and shooting training, Attacking down the middle, Opening the field from the goalie
Age level:	17 years - Adult
Level of play:	Advanced, Professional
Type of training:	Group training, Team training
Training structure:	Main point/Emphasis, End
Purpose:	Attack behavior, Groups, Improve individual skills
Total number of players:	10 or more players
Participating players:	Whole team
Training location:	Any
Spatial awareness:	Limited playing field
Duration:	10-20 min
Physiology:	Soccer-specific endurance, Explosiveness
Goalkeeping:	1 goalie

Organization:
Three cone goals are laid out as shown. Two or more players stand at the starting cones, two players stand at the middle cones and one player stands at the cone nearest to the goal. There is one goalkeeper in the goal.

Process:
The left and right groups take turns to complete the phases of play variation I & II culminating with a shot at the goal. The player passing the ball decides which variation he will run. The goalkeeper starts the move with a throw.

Variation I:
A (1) passes to C, B moves two to three meters to the side to be able to pass the ball from C to D with one touch. D attempts to score. A runs to the middle cone and B

takes up the positon from D. C stays at the middle cone. D joins the start cone etc.

Variation II:
Z passes (1) to X whose first movement is towards player Z. X (2) then lays the ball into space for Z and then moves after passing the ball. Z passes (3) to Y with his first touch, Y then passes with his first touch in space (4) to X. X passes to W (5). Player W tries to score. Z joins the middle cone after his pass. Y stays where he is. X joins the last cone with W after his three runs. W joins the start cone, etc.

Alternative:
- Goal scoring competition. Both teams count their goals scored.
- A second goal can be introduced.

Tip:

The focus is on a variation of fast passing combinations through the middle.

- Good technique, touch and passing is important.
- Strength and precision of the pass is important.
- Concentration must be held at all times.
- Communication is continuously important.
- Anticipation, awareness, reaction, speed of movement with and without the ball are regularly tested.
- Practice of rehearsed phases of play, short passing and variable combination soccer.
- Goal scoring.

Field size:
One half

Cone margins:
12 m

Materials:
1 normal goal, 6 cones

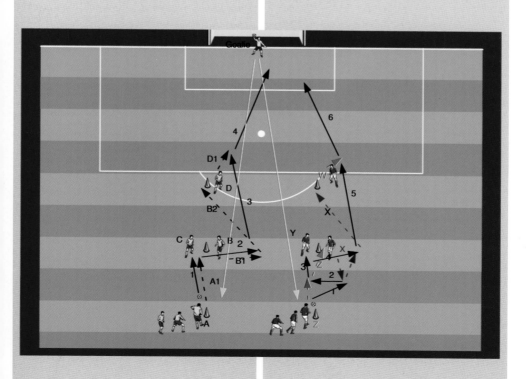

D. Brueggemann
Soccer Alive –
The Game is the Best Teacher

ISBN: 9781841262352
$ 19.95 US / $ 32.95 AUS
£ 12.95 UK / € 19.95

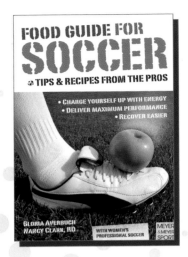

Gloria Averbuch & Nancy Clark, RD
Food Guide for Soccer -
Tips & Recipes from the Pros

ISBN 9781841262888
$ 18.95 US / $ 32.95 AUS
£ 14.95 UK / € 18.95

Gerhard Frank
Soccer Training Programs

ISBN: 9781841262741
$ 17.95 US / $ 29.95 AUS
£ 12.95 UK / € 16.95

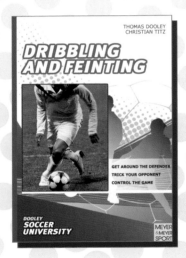

Dooley Soccer University
Thomas Dooley & Christian Titz
Dribbling & Feinting

ISBN: 9781841263014
$ 16.95 US/$ 29.95 AUS
£ 12.95 UK / € 16.95

Ralf Meier
Strength Training for Soccer

ISBN: 9781841262086
$ 16.95 US / $ 29.95 AUS
£ 12.95 UK / € 16.95

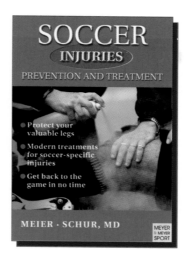

Ralf Meier/Andreas Schur, MD
Soccer Injuries

ISBN: 9781841262376
$ 16.95 US / $ 29.95 AUS
£ 12.95 UK / € 16.95

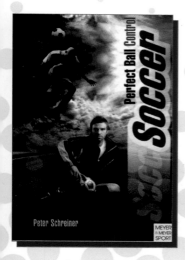

Peter Schreiner
Soccer – Perfect Ball Control

ISBN: 9781841262789
$ 16.95 US / $ 29.95 AUS
£ 12.95 UK / € 16.95

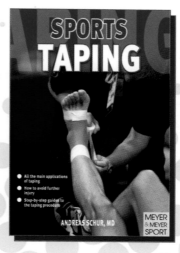

Andreas Schur, MD
Sports Taping

ISBN: 9781841262093
$ 16.95 US / $ 29.95 AUS
£ 12.95 UK / € 16.95

■ E-Mail
sales@m-m-sports.com

■ online
www.m-m-sports.com

■ Telephone / Fax
+49 2 41 - 9 58 10 -13
+49 2 41 - 9 58 10 -10

■ Mail
MEYER & MEYER Sport
Von-Coels-Str. 390, 52080 Aachen
Germany

**MEYER
& MEYER
SPORT**

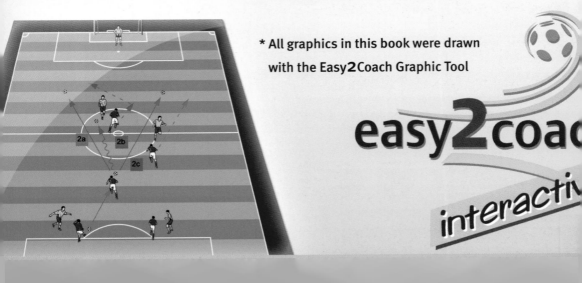

DOOLEY SOCCER UNIVERSITY

Official Soccer School since 2002

Dooley Soccer University with its unique modular concept is an in-
tionally oriented soccer service provider. It is our aim to serve the
s of different target groups with high quality products related to
er. The colourful world of soccer with all of its agents, on and off the
- we incorporate that into our daily work with everything we do.

OCCER SCHOOL (BASE TRAINING, CAMPS)

CONCEPT AND TRAINING INSTITUTE (USYS EUROPE, U 19 - BUNDESLIGA)

TRAINING PHILOSOPHY (BOOKS, E-BOOKS)

+ INTERNET PORTAL (EDUTAINMENT, VIDEOS, ONLINE-SHOP)

+ SOCIAL COMMITMENT (UNICEF, KEINE MACHT DEN DROGEN)

+ PROFESSIONAL NETWORK (CLUBS, INSTITUTIONS, PLAYERS)

+ PROJECTS (DEVELOPMENT OF CONCEPTS)

artners:

- WE BRING YOU TO THE NEXT LEVEL! -

WWW.DOOLEYSOCCER.US